Painted Turtle.
Painted Turtle Owners Manual.
Painted Turtle Pros and Cons, Care, Housing, Diet and Health.

by

David Donalton

Table of Contents

Introduction

Bringing home a turtle has more perks than one. For instance, it is only when you have a turtle at home that you can claim that you have a creature from the Jurassic era living in your home and not have people snickering at that. Turtles and tortoises have lived on earth for over 200 million years, meaning that they shared the earth with the mighty dinosaurs. Of course, today we view them as cute, shelled lovable beings but in reality they are living examples of Darwin's "Survival of the fittest" theory.

Domesticating animals has more meaning in the world today. It is not just about trading the animals or their products, it is about finding a friend for life. For many people they are replacements for having children of their own. They choose to bring home a pet and take care of it as their own baby. With the growing bond between pets and their owners, healthcare of pets has improved drastically including other conveniences like pet insurance. Of course, who can forget the incredible accessories and toys that we can provide for our little friends?

Given all that, the conventional choice for a pet would be a dog or a cat. But there are some who would like to invest in an exotic pet such as a turtle. Now, with exotic pets, there are a few more challenges as they need special care and a dedicated type of habitat to thrive in. Of course, there are more expenses involved. But most importantly, the legal considerations with respect to exotic pets like the turtle are a lot greater. To begin with not many species are permitted for domestication because of their endangered status. The good news is that there are over 300 species of turtles and tortoises that you can choose from to bring home as a pet. Make sure you are certain that your pet belongs to this category to avoid penalization.

The issue with pets like turtles is that certain buying and selling habits around the world have changed people's perception of the animal. For instance, on several beach locations, hermit crabs are sold as souvenirs or trinkets. What these vendors fail to tell the buyers is the exclusive habitat and the care that turtles require. Eventually, these turtles succumb to poor conditions and care. So, if you think that a turtle needs less care in comparison to dogs or cats, think again. This is especially for parents who want their children to have a low maintenance pet. A turtle is more high maintenance than you think.

Another issue with the turtle is the fact that they carry salmonella just like any other reptile or amphibian. That is why there are laws like the 4 inch law to protect the owners. This also means that the owners need to clean up the ecosystem of your turtle regularly in order to prevent any disease. Even the foods that you need to provide your turtle can be difficult to clean up. The chow that the turtles eat can increase the chances of any disease if you do not clean it up frequently. So you see, a tiny creature like the turtle can also mean a lot of responsibility.

These facts are only to help you realize that a turtle is a lot of work and you must be willing to invest some time in their care. The perks of having a turtle are at large. These creatures are extremely social and love to hang out with their owners. Now that does not mean that they like to cuddle. Handling can actually stress these creatures out a lot. Instead, you can watch them and interact with them with minimal handling. The thing with turtles is that they are not really meant for heavy petting.

But turtles can be fascinating creatures. Watching them interact with their tank mates, the way they bask in the lighting and also the way in which they feed can be cartloads of fun. It is a wonderful learning experience for children. They will be able to understand social interactions of animals and even get a good idea of group behavior from turtles.

Do they make great pets for children? After a certain age, yes. But you need to be very clear about the rules of hygiene and care. Salmonella is the biggest threat when it comes to turtles. So if you have young children at home, it is best not to leave them unsupervised with a turtle. But they can be a great way to teach children responsibility. The extensive set up and maintenance can be a fun family activity that will teach your children how to care for their pets, get into a good routine etc.

Although a turtle or a tortoise may look simple as a creature, the fact is that they are really complex organisms. They need dedicated care for a lifetime and their lifespans are also really long. Some of them live up to 50 years of age. So really think about getting yourself a turtle as a pet and ask yourself why you have opted for this creature over several others.

Chapter 1: Meet the Painted Turtle

One of the most colorful types of turtles, the painted turtle is one of the oldest species of turtles. The fossils of this species date back to almost 15 million years ago. Since then, these turtles have captured the interest of people and have been domesticated as pets.

The ChrysemysScriptaScripta, or Painted Turtle, is the only member of the Chrysemys family of turtles found around the world, and among the most common turtle breeds found in the United States of America. Poikilothermic by nature, these diurnal reptiles share such their natural habitat and many behavior traits with its American counterparts, the red-eared, yellow-bellied and Cumberland turtles.

It is the distinct vibrant coloring and pattern found on any of the four Painted turtle subspecies, along with its almost golden hue that gives the painted turtle its name. With a preference for freshwater aquatic spaces surrounding by soft, muddy banks in slightly warmer and regulated temperatures, the small-sized Painted turtles have been found to comfortably inhabit a large number of ecospaces, making them a popular choice among exotic pet enthusiasts.

1. Interaction of Painted Turtles with People

With small, vibrantly marked shell-encased bodies and a pleasing face, – it is not hard to see why humans would be immediately drawn towards painted turtles – or any of a variety of semi-aquatic chelonians, for that matter. While the relationship between turtles and humans dates back enough centuries to warrant their presence in local and traditional culinary and medicinal use as well as native Indian folklore, painted turtles found their place in the spotlight as popular pets in the 1900s.

First named ChrysemysPicta in early 1855 in the North American continent, the painted turtle was then classified into four sub-types in the following years, owing to a growing fascination among herpetological experts towards this chelonian. The subsequent discovery of the abundance of painted turtles in the wild, coupled with their relatively small size led to these reptiles finding a place in captivity with humans in the Americas. This trend caught on so quickly, that by the 1990s, painted turtles found themselves second in popularity as exotic pets only to the painted turtle, both within and outside the North American continent. Their consideration as attractive aquatic pets sold at reasonable rates also made them a staple at several county fairs, even giving rise to such activities as turtle racing.

As is inevitable with the attempted domestication of any previously untamed breed, however, the first breeders and farmers of Painted turtles as pets had little knowledge and resources to ensure proper sanitary care for these reptiles. An absence of awareness of the chelonian's food habits, behavioral patterns, life cycle and anatomical structure led to thousands of painted turtles being fed a diet too high in protein and comprising of offal as part of their upbringing. It comes as no surprise, then, that such unethical rituals resulted in the chelonians becoming carriers – and transmitters – of such lethal parasites as salmonella and bacteria Arizona.

In addition, the spread of salmonella by the turtles, another popular household reptilian pet, led to the passing of the 4-inch law, banning the sale of all turtles with a shell-diameter measuring less than 100 cm (4 inches) in the United States.

One of the most popular pets worldwide, painted turtles now found themselves unwanted as companions in captivity. In accordance with new laws, many painted chelonians found themselves re-thrust into the wild, forcing them to adapt to new ecosystems and breed with other turtle species such as the slider family. It is thanks to the readiness to breed, along with the relatively hardy disposition that painted turtles have managed to keep their numbers steady in the wild despite sharing a now-complicated relationship with human beings.

Residents, and the governments from this turtle's nonnative habitats (the rest of the North American continent and Europe), trying to control what would quickly become a dominant ecosystem member in such states as California, first classified the breed as an invasive species, then made several advancements to help prevent the spread of salmonella through vaccinations, sanitary housing, and proper food and health care. Owners and breeders, on the other hand, were given better training and education on how to properly care for exotic pets such as painted turtles.

It is around this time that the syndication of the popular children's cartoon "Teenage Mutant Ninja Turtles" came to everyone's rescue. Gaining widespread fame among adults and children for their quirky personalities and heroic archetypes, the fictional turtles brought about a renewed desire in the ownership of turtles as pets, with painted turtles being among those breeds that were most easily available in the local surroundings. They, thus, singlehandedly managed to bring about a resurgence in the sale of Painted turtles in the United States.

In today's times, the tumultuous relationship between painted turtles and human beings hangs on a precarious balance determined by the right kind of care, housing and healthcare provided to the turtles. This resurgence in sales coupled with a better knowledge on the care provided to reptiles in captivity has also proved to be useful to those farmers who ship painted turtles to south-east Asian countries for culinary, medicinal and religious purposes.

2. Natural Range and Habitat

In the Americas, you're most likely to find Painted turtles in abundance from the state of Alabama and Louisiana. The painted turtle is easily found in most of the counties in Canada, along with finding a healthy presence in several parts of Mexico as well. Within the United States of America, the painted turtle has comfortably settled among such states as Michigan, Oregon, California, North and South Carolina, Massachusetts, Georgia, New York, Kentucky, Illinois, Missouri and Arkansas, to name a few.

Across the ocean, painted turtles, though not native to this geography, continue to comfortably inhabit the vast expanse of the Eurasian region. Owing mostly to the practice of introducing these turtles into a new ecosystem in captivity, and then releasing them into the wild either upon dissatisfaction or by accident, expect to see lots of painted turtles in the Spain and Germany. As we move eastwards, Painted turtles once again become abundant in East Asia, in Japan, South Korea, Thailand, Guam and Israel.

3.   Painted Turtles and the Ecology

Painted turtles have managed to carve a unique and complicated existential zone within the ecology, thanks to their choice of habitat, behavioral patterns and feeding habits. Within the vast ecological space, painted turtles find themselves categorized with their small-sized counterparts that live in semi-aquatic conditions. In addition, painted turtles further slot themselves into a niche by being pond-dwelling, land-nesting reptiles of medium-size who are also omnivorous in nature. Within these parameters, however, painted turtles have found themselves contributing in ways that are critical to their non-native ecosystems.

Painted turtles, like all other living beings, play certain direct and indirect roles to help maintain ecological balance in their native space. Through such activities as foraging and breeding, these turtles not only take an active part in population control of several plant and animal species, but also contribute towards the growth of their own. Their vulnerability as eggs or hatchlings, along with their brumative state in the winter makes these medium-sized chelonians desired foods for larger animals like raccoons, foxes, birds of prey and other carnivorous turtles.

What complicates this terrapin's relationship with the ecology, however, is its existence and subsequent thriving in non-native habitats. Transported outside their native marshy habitat owing to growing popularity, painted turtles became a significant part of other terrains in the North-American continent, then crossing over to Europe, even Asia – a practice that led to several smaller-sized indigenous animal families falling prey to their dominant foraging and basking preferences. These hardy creatures were found to be adept at foraging for food, while capable of surviving cold winter conditions by entering a state of brumation.

To add to the growing list of ways by which painted turtles prove to be successful competitors in non-native territories, it is its nature as a chelonian that is believed to bring salmonella and other infections to those areas where it thrives. As a result, this subspecies of the terrapin family may not enjoy favor with several Wildlife authorities – a fact clearly emphasized by its inclusion on the list of invasive species in certain areas. Conversely, its status as the state reptile of some areas in North America has lent the painted turtle the label of a prized and even endangered species of turtle, meant for preservation and promotion. This conflicting attitude of humans towards the painted turtles, depending on the areas they inhabit, perhaps contributes most greatly towards its role in its surrounding ecology.

We know today, that proper care, sanitation practices and a controlled environment can help painted turtle thrive in captivity, and prevent them from spreading infectious illnesses. Their negative impact in certain non-native environments, however, has been felt to an extent that has forced several governments to make the choice to discourage their survival, rather than preserve it.

4.   Breed Characteristics and Appearance

An adult painted turtle is a small-sized member of the pond-slider family, usually growing to a shell length up to 10 inches (25 cm), settling in at a weight in the range of 200 and 500 gms. A healthy painted adult is often classified by the above optimum shell length and weight, along with four other important characteristic physical traits:

1) a wide stripe behind the eye area in hues of yellow with a yellow-striped face,

2) a distinct V-shaped yellow notch meeting at the jawline,

3) a smoothly-textured oval-shaped olive to black shell carapace (top part of the shell) with groove-like markings,

4) and prominent yellow or red plastron (bottom shell) hue with visible markings adding vibrancy to its appearance.

Adult male painted turtles have been studied to grow to a size comparably smaller to their female counterparts. With an average shell-size of 4 to 8 inches, adult males red-eared terrapins are also told apart from females through such markers as longer, more curved claws used for mating, a longer and prominently thicker tail and the farther position of their cloaca from the carapace than female painted turtles. The females, on the other hand, possess wider bodies and a heavier weight, both aiding in carrying a large clutch of eggs.

Painted turtles have an average life expectancy of around 20 to 30, even 50 years in the wild, sometimes living for a shorter period in captivity. As part of this considerably long lifespan, painted turtles develop at their own pace, reaching full maturation and adulthood between the ages of 2 and 4 years for males, and 6 to 10 years for females, depending on the subspecies and size of the shell.

Sex determination and the painted turtle

While there may be certain characteristic features that differentiate adult male painted turtles from the females, these distinctions are only prominent once the turtles have attained sexual maturity. Unlike several other species, painted turtles possess an anatomy whose gender-distinct sexual maturity is governed by the dimensions of its shell in the males, and its age in years in the females.

It is also a unique phenomenon that plays a part in sex determination among painted turtles. As with their slider turtle counterparts, the sex in painted terrapins is determined at the incubation stage. Regardless of the dominance of chromosomes at the time of embryonic development, the sex of the painted turtle is determined by the ambient temperature of its incubation setting.

While male painted turtles are guaranteed to be born in temperatures ranging between 23 and 29 degrees Celsius, female painted turtles can be hatched by incubating the eggs in temperature of 29 to 31 degrees Celsius. To further add to the uniqueness of the sex determine phenomenon, incubating the eggs at the median temperature can also successfully breed transgender hatchlings – resulting in a high success rate with breeding endeavors in a controlled environment.

5. Different Types of Painted Turtles

1. Name: Eastern Painted

Official Name: ChrysemysPictaPicta
Natural Range: Georgia, North and South Carolina, Virginia, Maryland, Delaware, New Jersey, Connecticut, Rhode Island, Massachusetts, New Hampshire, Vermont, Maine, Nova Scotia, New BrunswickDelaware, New Jersey, Connecticut, Rhode Island, Massachusetts, New Hampshire, Vermont, Maine, Nova Scotia, New BrunswickDelaware, New Jersey, Connecticut, Rhode Island, Massachusetts, New Hampshire, Vermont, Maine, Nova Scotia, New Brunswick
Appearance (Shell):
Carapace: olive green to black, pale stripe down the center, red markings along edges. Scutes: pale-colored edges occurring in straight rows

Plastron: plain yellow, may be lightly spotted with grey
Scutes: pale-colored edges occurring in straight rows
Plastron: plain yellow, may be lightly spotted with grey
Adult Size: 13-17 cm (5-7in)
Food Habits: Largely aquatic plants and injured/dead fish.

2. Name: Western Painted
Official name: ChrysemysPictaBellii
Natural range: New Mexico, Texas, Arizona, Colorado, Utah, Oregon, Canada, Illinois, Michigan, Wisconsin, North and South Dakota, Missouri, Nebraska, Kansas, Oklahoma, Montana.
Appearance (shell): Carapace: olive-green to black, central strip may be faint or absent
Scutes: lightly striped mesh-like patterns, pale-colorededges occurring in alternating segments
Plastron: brightly colored patch spreading from the center to the edges.
Adult size: 10-26.6 cm (4-10in)
Food habits: Seasonally varied diet: 60% insects (summer), 55% plants (winter)

3. Name: Midland Painted
Official name: ChrysemysPictaMarginata
Natural range: Ontario, Quebec, Kentucky, Tennessee, Alabama, West Virginia, Maryland, Pennsylvania, New York, Vermont
Appearance (shell): Carapace: olive-dull green, central strip may be absent
Scutes: very lightly striped mesh-like patterns, pale-colored segments occurring in alternating segments
Plastron: shadowy-grey patch on yellow surface usually around the center
Adult size: 10-26.6 cm (4-10 in)
Food habits: Largely aquatic plants, weeds, algae

4. Name: Southern Painted
Official name: ChrysemysPictaDorsalis

Natural range: Illinois, Missouri, Mississippi river valley, Arkansas, Texas, Oklahoma, Louisiana, gulf of Mexico, Tennessee, Alabama

Appearance (shell): Carapace: olive green to black, prominent red stripe down the center and red edges Scutes: pale-colored edges occurring in alternating segments Plastron: darker yellow or tan, may be lightly or not spotted at all

Adult size: 10-14 cm (4-6 in)

Food habits: Chronologically varied diet: 13% vegetarian (juvenile), 88% vegetarian (adult)

6. Behavior of the Painted Turtle

Normally, painted turtles are quite sociable in nature. However, the behavior of these turtles changes quite drastically depending upon the environment. They do not have any aggressive defense mechanism and are considered to be quite harmless.

The painted turtles, depending on the time of year and their level of interaction with other animals, possess a varied range of behavioral patterns that make them interesting to observe, both in the wild and in captivity. While part of their own genus, painted turtles display many behavioral traits similar to the slider turtle family, a family of chelonians who frequently inhabit the same ecospaces as our painted terrapin friends. Painted turtles are often singled out – apart from their appearance – by such common behaviors as basking, nesting, brumating, and displaying unique mating rituals coupled with aggressive behavior.

Painted turtles, while being largely hostile towards other species and humans, show fairly sociable natures that encourage interaction with other pond-sliders. Preferring to rest alone at night, but bask together during the day, adult painted turtles share such duties as feeding, basking and mating, while sparing no attention towards caring for the young. While some painted settlements may be small in size, their love for basking at optimal spots in their natural setting means that you can easily spot a group of over 10 or 20 painted turtles basking while stacked atop each other near pond or lake clearings.

Basking in particular, seems to be a preferred behavioral trait among several all pond-sliding species, let alone the painted turtle

- not only has this practice found to be healthy for the upkeep of the reptile's shell and body temperature, but it has also been observed to provide a deep sense of pleasure to the chelonians themselves. So great is the pleasure derived during basking rituals, that other smaller animals may often be aggressively chased away from prized basking zones. Not particularly known for their sensory abilities, painted turtles are believed to possess poor hearing, making up for this deficit with sharper responses to vibrations in the environment. This ability to sense vibrations helps them stay alert even while basking or napping underwater. With no designated space reserved for sleep and rest during the darker hours of the day, painted turtles spend their sleeping hours floating gently across the water, usually in secluded and hidden areas with plenty of protective yet soft cover.

Owing to their small size compared to larger animals in the ecosystem, painted turtles will rarely attempt to confront their predators or sources of threat, choosing instead to evade capture by abruptly sliding into the water or retreating into their shell. While a successful means of evasion in the wild, this startled reaction in a captive setting often proves stressful to the terrapin's health.

Chapter 2: Considerations before Bringing Home a Painted Turtle

Like any other species of turtles, painted turtles are quite the responsibility. From large tanks, to special lighting to veterinary charges, you have to take care of several nuances when you bring home a turtle. These creatures require a special type of ecosystem to thrive. In fact for every inch of the turtle, you require 10 gallons of water. That is the amount of work involved with these creatures. So, before you bring home a turtle, ask yourself the following questions:

1.   Are you ready for a Life Long Commitment?

By nature, painted turtles are known to be inquisitive and aggressive, with a desire for wandering about the places in search of food and water. This inquisitive nature, however, should not be mistaken for friendliness; many terrapins may take weeks, even months to domesticate. Until you can build a relationship of trust with your pet, the painted turtle will possibly repel any efforts at being touched, held or grabbed. With slightly temperamental personalities and reptilian thought processes, painted turtles may also never entirely become comfortable around your presence, and may have to be left undisturbed.

Their attractive features, content behavior while swimming and basking, and pleasing, almost smirking appearance may cheat many hopeful caregivers into believing that painted turtles require little to no monitored care in order to thrive. These chelonians, however, have been categorized as exotic pets with sound reason. An exotic animal is so labelled when it demands particular care, housing and handling methods for its survival – painted turtles fulfil these fundamentals by needing voluminous tanks to swim, bask, feed and burrow in, a varied diet to sustain their health, and deliberate behavioral and medical treatment.

Despite their independent natures, however, painted turtles can also be needy once they bond with their caregivers and distinguish them as primary sources of food. In the wild, these terrapins rely on available resources in nature for nutrition and shelter. With timely feeding routines, and a tendency to beg for food that is dense in protein, it becomes the caregiver's obligation to make certain that the dietary needs of their pets are met, as well as controlled. Care also needs to be taken on behalf of the painted turtle to make certain that all essentials in the housing zone are well-suited with the turtle's health and safety.

Apart from providing conditions that encourage physical wellbeing, painted turtles also need daily stipulated time for basking and swimming in order to thrive, with special conditions made for their comfort during the winter months. Periods of extended neglect towards such duties as regular cleaning and filtration of water, or cleaning away of food and excrement particles may make your turtle mortally ill, or may cause it distress.

Painted turtles are also diurnal in nature, and are active for about 17 hours of the day. In order to successfully build a bond with your painted turtle, you will have to make certain that your daily schedules correspond with the waking hours of your pet, while still catering them with the privacy they may demand during basking or feeding; should you work during the day, it may be best to consider nocturnal pets such as Tiger Salamanders.

If the demanding standards necessitated by these chelonians cannot be met, it is best to re-think your decision to house painted turtles, whether for companionship or consequent profit. On the other hand, if you maintain a lifestyle that can comfortably integrate a pet as demanding yet detached as the painted turtle, you may find that they make for entertaining and rewarding lifelong pets.

2.   Will they make good pets for kids?

We have already discussed how these chelonians, as exotics, need a particular method of caregiving that addresses their food, health, habitat and emotional needs. The child will also need to put in the obligatory bonding time needed to tame the turtle and make it comfortable around its presence. Since the process of acquainting oneself with a reptile can take days, even weeks to accomplish, a child may quickly become impatient, when an adult would understand the time needed to do the same.

It is probably due to their misleadingly pleasing appearance, along with their illustration in the media as lovable cartoon or wise storybook characters, that painted turtles are believed to be suitable pets for people of all ages. If you are bringing a painted turtle to a house that has children, or plan to gift one to a young child, however, you should take the time to consider that this may not be the wisest idea.

While it is definitely not true for all children, younger caregivers may not always form a friendly and caring relationship with their painted turtles. This unlikelihood can largely be credited to the violent and often distant personalities of the average painted turtle, and the easiness with which children can become bored of carrying out ritualistic duties.

Due to their hatred of being held or handled - at least primarily - children may find themselves being regularly nipped or scratched at when they try to grab their chelonian pets. Many children may additionally be disgusted by slippery feel of a turtle's body. Again, a reasonable adult, or even child, should know that these reptiles only bite as an act of defence, but many children tend to process the attack as an act of open aggression. This may lead to the child either abandoning the pet for fear of being bitten again, or may trigger the child's anger and cause them to hurt the pet by way of payback.

If your pet turtle is relatively tame and can socialize comfortably with children, it becomes your duty to make sure that the turtle is handled the correct way. With slithery skin and a wriggly nature, painted turtles can be easily dropped if not held with proper care. Furthermore, while a child may want to squeeze the pet in their palms as a sign of affection, they may not realize the result of their actions. If left unattended in a tank with no covering, painted turtles will gladly climb out of their housing spaces, getting lost as a result of long wandering or becoming an easy target for larger predators. Painted turtles are not the type of domestic pet that can be handled without extreme caution exercised on the owner's part. With a disposition towards carrying and spreading salmonella at any point in their lives, daily handling of a painted turtle requires rough and thorough washing and sterilizing of hands, clothes and items that come into contact with the pets. Any missed chance at cleaning up may potentially expose your children to a salmonella infection at worst. With their notorious status as an aggressive biological species, should your child find themselves unhappy with their pet, several local laws will prevent you from setting the painted terrapin back into the wild – making the pet your lifelong responsibility.

It is not just young children, but also teenagers who are generally advised against housing painted turtles, if they cannot provide the demanding care the exotics need. A spacious housing facility with provisions for an earthly as well as aquatic setting, a steady routine that complements the chelonians lifestyle and a stable income are the basics for purchasing a painted turtle as a pet - factors that children, teenagers, students and unemployed or lower-income group members are often not able to fulfil. If the terrapin is housed in such cramped spaces as dormitory rooms or bathroom shelves, and is left abandoned during its feeding and cleaning periods, it can become easily stressed, develop behavioural disorders, fall ill or even drown.

This does not mean that children and teenagers are to be completely banned from raising or handling painted turtles. It is simply important that you, as a responsible caregiver, teach younger members on the right ways to interact with and care for these pets before you consider bringing them home. Being aware of the difference between an exotic and a common household pet such as dog or cat, can go a long way in preparing younger children to live with the challenging, but fascinating painted turtle.

3.   What are the costs involved?

It is a misguided conception that a small, semi-aquatic pet such as a painted turtle will not need too much money to either bring home or raise. In truth, any exotic, let alone a turtle, can make a considerable dent in your monthly savings, by way of upkeep and maintenance. Your pet will need particular living conditions, food and medical attention to live; in addition, the longevity of their lifespan demands that you provide these demanding conditions for approximately 30 years at least. This makes it vital for you to consider whether you can afford to raise and care for a painted turtle.

As a possible caregiver, you will first need to invest approximately USD 400 to 700 (around 265 to 465 British pounds) to create a set-up for your painted turtle. Depending on the number of turtles you plan to bring home, an average-sized tank with a 60-gallon capacity and no extra attachments will cost you between 150 and 450 USD (100-300 British pounds).

This price does not include the inner necessary elements that make up an ideal environment for your pet. You will have to provide tank furnishings and flooring elements, such as water filters and heaters, UVA and UVB lighting fixtures, lamp reflectors and thermometers. For their basking needs, your housing should also include a basking platform along with heat lamps as a backup basking measure.

Other essentials in the tank will include materials that make up the substrate, aquatic plants, water testing and treatment kits, etc. This phase of preparing the habitat should set you back by an additional 150 to 300 USD (100-200 British pounds), but can also amount to a larger sum, depending on the number of elements and excellence of elements you add to the tank.

The next financial concerns should be made towards the food you provide your pets with. Your painted turtles, especially if brought home as hatchlings, will need a steady diet of nutritious food, in the form of protein, pellets and mineral supplements. As they settle into a routine with you, you can keep a watch on their feeding habits and adjust their food based on their individual habits. To start, apart from prepared commercial food at 10 USD (6 British pounds) per can, stocking up on food for your grown pets will cost you at least 40 USD (25 British pounds) a month for fruits and vegetables, with live food and supplements adding another 30 to 40 USD (20-25 British pounds) to your budget. This cost will likely vary depending on the food preferences and growth of your painted turtles.

None of the above expenses even begin to cover the healthcare your painted terrapins will need, from the brief starter visit to the exotic pet expert and vaccinations, which are estimated to cost between 80 and 120 USD (50-80 British pounds). Regular monthly check-ups can run a yearly bill ranging between 20 and 100 USD (15-60 British pounds), and a probable surgical procedure or laboratory test will cost an additional 100 to 200 USD (60-140 British pounds). It is only once these primary arrangements are made can you consider the actual cost of a pet painted turtle.

The average cost of purchasing this popular terrapin ranges from 10 USD (6 British pounds) for painted turtles to upwards of 50 USD (30 British pounds), depending on the source your pet is acquired from, and the genetics of the turtle itself. Private breeders and fanciers are known for raising friendlier and healthier turtles than their store-bought equivalents – but they also cost more than the latter.

Many pet painted turtles are sold by breeders and fanciers who offer to ship the pets to locations that allow the ownership of these exotics. Since the United States is the most popular source for reputed painted turtle breeders, your shipping fees, depending on your location and that of your seller, may add anything from 30

USD to 75 USD (20-50 British pounds) to your primary investment.

For a healthy quality of life that is neither too sparse nor too extreme for the turtles, you should be prepared to part with about 700-1500 USD (450-1000 British pounds) as a primary investment for a pair of Painted turtles, and then budget around 150 to 200 USD (65-140 British pounds) every month for habitat upkeep, activities such as basking and bromating, food and healthcare.

4.   Are there any legal considerations?

For those who like the unique and possibly detached perspective on domestication that painted turtles have to offer, the chelonians make for easy-to-please, laidback companions. If you have already decided that this terrapin is your pet of choice, you may also take a special interest in the process through which your painted turtle reaches you. Vast though their natural range may be, not all painted turtles are up for picking and housing at the individual's will.

The invasive nature of a couple of subspecies from this family – along with the endangered status they are given in some areas – accompanied by their status as carriers of salmonella, means that they receive special regulation across the North American, Australian and European continents. While some of these rules lay certain restrictions on the purchase and possession of these chelonians, other laws may prohibit the acquisition or probable release into the wild of any painted turtles altogether. Therefore, in order to protect yourself, is it essential that you have some clarity on the legality behind buying and owning a painted turtle.

It wouldn't be surprising if you had your heart set on owning a painted turtle. You must know, however, that selling, buying, possessing and releasing any of these chelonians is illegal in Florida, and is governed by strict regulations in several other states whose local plant and animal life have been negatively impacted by its population. If you live in Indiana, it helps to know that it is only a group of lobbyists who have been able to temporarily thwart the decision to outlaw these terrapins from the state altogether.

If you do live in a North American state that permits you to house a painted turtle, you may find yourself turning to the legal pages once again, should you make certain decisions regarding your pet's development. Certain activities, such as the breeding, sale of eggs or hatchlings, or even releasing a captive terrapin into the wild can be met with severe penalties – either a fine, imprisonment, or both.

Furthermore, the extent of invasiveness of this species in such non-native areas as Europe and Australia have forced them to deem the import of the painted turtles illegal without the necessary permits and licenses. Harsh penalties for its illegal import have been accompanied by ongoing awareness programs on this subject.

To make matters more complicated, should you choose to simply go looking for painted turtle eggs or hatchlings in the wild, or give a home to a lost pet, ensure that you are legally permitted to do so. Many states prohibit their residents to adopt painted turtles, owing to the complications behind rehabilitating a chelonian, and for fear of the owner contracting salmonella, or releasing the pet back into the wild.

The question then arises, "can I legally own a painted turtle at all in the United States?" If you're willing to be diligent about adhering to local wildlife laws, in many areas, you most certainly can. A quick perusal of the local Game and Wildlife laws that govern each county or state reveals it is only those areas most severely impacted by the introduction of the red-eared terrapin into their native ecosystem that have specific guidelines dictating the terms of their sale, acquisition or ownership.

Therefore, while you still may not be able to either bring home or raise a painted turtle in the states of Florida and Oregon, you most certainly can give a home to at least one or two chelonians in other North American states, Canada and Europe – so long as they aren't imported. Consider your purchase as a way of providing long-term help to check the population of invasive species in your local ecosystem, and you may find that owning a painted turtle is not that tricky a process to navigate.

If you aren't sure whom to ask for the right legal information concerning the acquisition and ownership of painted turtles as pets, you can find plenty of literature on this subject on the Internet. Each state's government website lists out all particulars surrounding the purchase and possession of its local flora and fauna. Browse through the Game and Wildlife department pages for the most accurate and up-to-date information.

The link between salmonella, the pet turtle trade and the 4-inch law:

When we mention the purchase of painted turtles for domestication in the United States of America, a discussion on the 4-inch law, its history, need and contemporary relevance is inevitable. A law put into place by the United Stated Food and Drug Administration in 1975, the 4-inch remains a controversial and highly debated subject among naturists, chelonian breeds and individual owners.

To explain the 4-inch law in a nutshell, the sale of painted turtles with a carapace-length of under 4 inches (100 cm) is prohibited across the United States. This law was considered necessary after the overwhelming sale of this terrapin from the 1900s to the 1960s, coupled with insufficient knowledge on the care of the reptile, led to a deadly spread of salmonella among citizens, particularly children. It was determined that the younger hatchlings with their smaller shell-length could easily fit into children's mouths, giving the children salmonella through casual contact.

A better awareness in today's times on the raising of these turtles, on the other hand, has led to sharp decline in cases related to salmonella contraction from painted turtles. Better healthcare, housing facilities and an awareness of the right hygiene while handling the chelonians has raised several questions on the contemporary relevance of this law. Younger and smaller painted turtles are no more of a salmonella hazard than their adult counterparts, and both groups can be successfully housed provided basic cleanliness rituals are followed.

5. The right age and gender to bring home Painted Turtles – and how many?

Once you have guaranteed yourself – through satisfactory research and homework – of the legality of bringing home a painted turtle in your geographic location, you can begin to think about the specifics of your pet. Many possible terrapin owners often find themselves disagreeing between the choice to bring home fully-grown adult painted turtles or raise baby hatchlings into adults. Your final decision should be one that addresses the purposes behind bringing home your chelonian. .

The first aspect to bear in mind is the nature of your pet, regardless of their age; painted turtles live out their existence on two surfaces – water as well as land, requiring both in equal measure to thrive. As the caregiver of a creature whose life cycles regulate such basic activities as breathing, nutrient absorption and foraging for food, you have to be ready to guide your pet through each developmental stage.

You then turn to address the purpose of the new pet in your household - are they your first chelonian or turtle, or are they brought to add to an already prevailing community? If this is your first experience with handling and caring for exotic reptiles, it may be desirable to bring adult turtles, and care for the young when consequent eggs are laid.

This does not mean that young painted turtles should not be considered at the time of purchase - simply that they require more exacting care than their adult counterparts. If you happen to acquire, or wish to purchase painted turtles, therefore, it is best that you make preparations for an aquatic habitat with a selected dry area for basking, vital for younger hatchling development. A largely protein-rich carnivorous diet, the right temperature settings and privacy should help your young one grow into a beautiful sexually mature adult within 2-7 years, depending on the gender.

It must be remembered, however, that the 4-inch law that limits the sale of turtles in the United States may either make it legally difficult, or next-to-impossible to bring home a young painted turtle. If you find yourself faced with no choice but to bring home a maturing or fully-matured adult painted terrapin, you can still enjoy a lasting and fulfilling relationship with the pet, so long as you can cater lasting care and attention.

If you already have your own community of painted turtles at home, hatchlings may not easily blend into an already changed environment. An adult community of painted terrapins require an adult to properly adapt to the generally aggressive commencement ritual and consequent competition for food and mates. While your society of painted turtles may avoid and even bully younger hatchlings, they are more likely to treat an adult of similar size with higher acceptance.

The true predicament in bringing home an unsociable painted terrapin lies in the ultimate need to provide it with a partner. While not particularly determined on breeding or reproducing, painted turtles have been studied to thrive emotionally when provided with at least one another's companion. Whether of balancing or contrasting genders, it is the social interaction that keeps the turtles from unveiling highly fearful and violent behaviour patterns.

As an unprofessional breeder, it would be best to begin with one turtle, and work your way towards investing in a tank mate; should you have the resources and patience, however, consider bringing home a pair from the get go. Apart from the slight increase in your primary investments, you will have a higher probability of bringing home pets that get along.

As with many animal species, a male and female adult would ideally do well if housed together. Two males may only compete during the rare feeding or basking routine, and a pair of females have been studied to get along marvellously. In case of a community setting, however, it may be best to either have a larger number of females in the tank, or house the males and females separately at the time of breeding and mating to avoid competitive or sexually violent behaviour towards each other.

No matter what the age of the painted turtle you finally do bring home, it is important that the animal be in as healthy a state as possible. Have your reptile tested for salmonella and any other existing medical conditions, and give the primary period of at least 30 days in isolation, until they get used to their surroundings.

6. What are The Pros and Cons of Painted turtle ownership

Pros of Painted turtle ownership

As an exotic semi-aquatic aggressive species, painted turtles may not have the universal plea that dogs and cats command as prized pets. They demand challenging living, behaviour, diet and health conditions in order to thrive, and take comparatively longer to tame than other popular pet species. For those who follow a routine that complements the animal's quotidian natures and can make the commitment, however, raising pet painted terrapins can turn into a beneficial and rewarding experience. Despite their slightly distant natures, painted turtles can be advantageous to their caregivers in the following ways:

● Diurnal by nature, painted turtles are active by day and asleep during the night hours, making them easy to bond with if you work from home or are free during the daytime.

● While in their tank, they are fast and flexible swimmers and avid baskers, making them entertaining to watch. They can be tamed to an extent and once you build a bond with your terrapins, you can also expect them to be approachable to your presence.

● The most popular pet among the semi-aquatic turtle family after Red-eared slider turtles, painted turtles have upheld interactions with humans since the 1900s, making them relatively friendlier towards humans other turtle species.

● Painted turtles may grow to a size of up to 8 inches, but are also among the smaller-size of the semi-aquatic and basking turtle family. If you are looking to tame a turtle that does not demand overly large enclosures and too much space, the painted turtle would be a better option than the yellow-bellied slider or cooter turtle.

● With a need for a precise temperature and habitat setting that can be provided in an enclosed space through such simple devices as water heaters and basking lamps, you can comfortably house painted turtles through a variety of climatic conditions.

● Depending on the hygiene standards and housing you provide, painted turtles can be hardy little creatures, with immune systems that can fight several infections - health problems, if any, will often result from shell-related illnesses, or wounds and bites continued from injuries.

● For those looking to bring home a pet that does not need extreme handling and is meant for decorative purposes, the Painted turtle is an attractive and non-threatening option when compared to such exotic pets as snakes, lizards and certain frogs, and adds an elegant touch to the spaces it occupies.

• For those looking to bring home a pet that can be housed inside an aquarium, painted turtles make for a longer-living and hardier option than most freshwater fish, while also being more responsive than several popular pet fish species.

•Painted turtles are also an excellent option for those people looking to provide a home for a banished or neglected exotic pet – you can find plenty of healthy painted turtles up for adoption at veterinary amenities, re-homing and animal rescue centres.

• With a preference for privacy and relative seclusion, painted turtles do not require daily attachment and playtime in order to thrive. As long as you can provide food, clean water and optimal basking conditions on a daily basis, your painted turtles will not demand extra attention from you – making them a better option than such pets as chipmunks or dogs.

• When compared to many other pets, painted turtles live a moderately long life of 20 to 50 years in captivity, sometimes even making it for over half a century! This longevity of existence makes them ideal pet for those who become quickly attached to their pets and are looking for lifetime domestic friendship.

Cons of painted turtle ownership

Among those who have not raised a turtle, cold-blooded or aquatic pet, or any type of exotic before, it is a common misunderstanding that these chelonians with a pleasing facade are low-maintenance and need little care. This protected notion, however, could not be further from the truth. As is common with all exotics, painted turtles, too, display behavior patterns that are different from other conservative pets such as dogs, cats, rabbits or horses. They are less likely to adapt their lifestyle to suit yours; rather it is you whose timetable will have to complement the terrapin's in order for it to survive. As sociable as they can be in the home of the right owner, here are some of the ways through which painted turtles could become a disadvantage to unprepared or reluctant owners:

• Painted turtles are not needy, but can be highly dependent on their caregiver as pets. Apart from timely feeding and health check-ups, you will also have to dedicate planned time on a daily, weekly and monthly basis towards cleaning their enclosure.

• While content to be among their kind as adults, they demand a high level of attention from caregivers as hatchlings. The process of hatchling painted eggs, as well as caring for them through their first year requires patience and meticulousness.

• Even though they depend on their caregiver for food, basking and hygienic housing in captivity, painted turtles are independent by nature, desiring to be touched or held only when they please. You may spend hours each day caring for and watching your Painted turtles, and the chelonian may still be opposed to your touch, or may fight back when being held.

• Painted turtles may be content to be housed within a controlled environment, but are also reasonably messy animals who will dirty their surroundings on a daily basis. You will need to make facilities for daily water cleaning, spot-cleaning and habitat renovating on a regular basis to prevent infections and disease from soiling the housing.

• Personality-wise, painted turtles can become self-protective during such times as feeding, mating or nesting, towards their tank mates as well as their caregivers. Pet owners often tell stories of their pets regularly demonstrating varying degrees of dominance and violence towards other mates or the caregiver themselves, based on their individual personalities.

• Painted turtles are known to bite, kick or scratch other tank mates, or even their caregiver. It must be noted, however, that these pets will infrequently bite without reason - if they do, it is most often an instinctive response to be held or touched.

• If you are looking for a pet who can be limited to the boundaries of their tank without added security measures, do not be fooled by the painted turtle's laid-back attitude and small size.

Inquisitive by nature, they will wander off if their tanks or housing is left unlocked or uncovered. They are also prized targets for common predators found in an urban setting and can easily be attacked by a dog, cat, fox, snake or even another large turtle.

●Painted turtles can also be stubborn pets who are not concerned about instructions, making their training somewhat difficult and tiring for the caregiver.

● Requiring continuous monitoring of their habitat, along with scheduled cleaning, caring for painted turtles can limit such activities as taking holidays or long trips away from home, unless a substitute caregiver is found.

● With such needs as water purification devices, basking zones and lamps, water heating products and regular upkeep of enclosure, providing an ideal setting for your painted turtles can quickly become a costly affair, making them an unfitting option for those on a tight budget.

● If you are unsure of the caregiver's capabilities or preference to care for a pet for at least 20 years, the longevity of this chelonians life may be a disadvantage to such possible owners as children.

● Their status as aggressive species and the validities placed on the breeding, sale and release of painted turtles in the wild makes it difficult for painted turtles to be re-homed in case you find yourself dumbfounded by the expenses and time that they take up.

7. Other Questions to Ask Yourself

A variety of factors come into play when deciding whether a painted turtle - or two - will be suitable as a pet for you. We have already discussed, at length, the amount of considerations you are needed to make as a caregiver - from understanding the legal and social insinuations of housing this aggressive terrapin species, to learning what caring for this reptile truly involves. In order to properly summarize all the prerequisites that are best fulfilled before purchasing a painted turtle, here is a checklist of questions to ask yourself:

• Can you comfortably set aside between 800 and 1500 USD (5000-1000 British pounds) every year for the care and maintenance of your pet?

• Can you fulfil all the legal fundamentals placed by your local authorities before owning a painted turtle?

• Can you comfortably and steadily source and provide live food, plant matter, vegetables and water that is clean and filtered and changed regularly?

• Can you locate a reputed and trustworthy exotic pet care expert/veterinarian in your area for your chelonian?

• Can you capably make the place within the housing zone ideal for your painted terrapin, with allocated areas for swimming, basking, feeding and burrowing?

• Can you efficiently make the premises outside the tank "predator-and-injury-proof" before it's time to let your painted turtle out for optional sunlight and exercise?

• Can you faithfully spare time once a day to spot clean the tank, and then clear time once or twice a month for a complete clean-up and renovation?

• Can you be tolerant and handle being constantly nipped, kicked or scratched - especially during the first few weeks?

• Can you dedicate sufficient time and space on a daily basis towards basking and swimming for its development and wellbeing?

• Can you live with a chelonian who may develop an aggressive personality, or who may detest being touched or handled?

- Can you comfortably handle a turtle when it becomes erratic and calm it down?

- Are you ready to handle violent impulses, antisocial phases or an uncaring attitude from your pets, especially during the winter and breeding months?

- Can you quickly spot and address any health-related issues that many gather up in your painted turtle?

- Can you either prevent or control breeding among your painted turtles, or provide a home for all resulting hatchlings?

- Can you provide care for your pet from a responsible person in your absence?

- Are you comfortable with caring for a pet for at least 20 and maybe up to 50 or more years?

- Can you provide devoted care for the pet throughout its lifespan, without exposing it to the wild or giving it up for adoption?

No matter how the above list of questions may guide your ultimate decision, finally, bringing home a painted turtle should be a decision that enriches the lives of both, the amphibian, and you.

Chapter 3: Bringing Home your Painted Turtle

When you are purchasing a painted turtle, you need to be sure of the breed that you are bringing home. If you are not sure of the breed specifications, your breeder could be selling you just about any species and passing it off as a painted turtle. The fear is not bringing home a wrong species. The fear is bringing home an illegal one. If you have decided to bring home a painted turtle despite all the considerations mentioned in the previous chapter, you need to read this chapter very carefully.

1. Checking the Health of your Painted Turtle

Once you have put careful thought into the outcomes that bringing home a painted turtle can have, it is best to find the right sources to purchase your pet from. Buying a painted turtle takes more effort than walking into a shop and selecting the prettiest reptile on a whim; a variety of factors finalise whether the painted turtle on offer is in good enough condition to take home with you. When you set out to buy a painted turtle, aim to return with the healthiest terrapin of the bunch. You can only receive a complete bill of health from your local chelonian expert, but a few simple physical indicators should reveal the state of health of your potential painted turtle:

1.   The eyes of the painted turtle should be clear, and not clouded over, hollow or oozing any liquids,

2.   A healthy painted turtle hatchling can walk almost immediately after it hatches, and swim 21 days after hatching. Any hatchling that is indolent or inert is unhealthy,

3.   The painted turtle should either be actively swimming and basking during the day hours, not resting or floating listlessly around the tank; any irregular motor movement indicates injury, even distortion,

4.   The shell should be smooth, lengthened and have a keel in the centre; any cracks, mouldy growth, foul smell or bleeding is an indication of lethal injury.

5.   A healthy painted turtle will continuously look for food sources; lack of appetite is an indicator of poor health,

6.   While painted turtles are messy, they are not unsanitary. If the potential painted turtle is covered in his own faecal matter, which is alarmingly smelly, or is covered in mites, the painted turtle is not healthy.

7.   Ensure that the nose is not runny or swollen, as this may indicate an infection that the painted turtle will carry for life and possibly spread to other turtles.

8.   Finally, check the painted turtle for visible injuries, scars, sores or wounds. Only if the painted turtle can clear all of your health inspections should you ask the vendors for the price.

2.   Buying from a Vendor

The most easily available source of painted turtles for purchase are reputed and licensed pet stores in your area. Painted turtles available at these stores are often sold at a lower rate than other sources such as breeders and fanciers, often because they have been attained in large numbers at wholesale rates, or possibly even rescued from adoption homes. Many stores also have online portals that allow you to choose and have your painted turtle shipped to your location for an extra charge.

Painted turtles acquired from pet stores may also not be as friendly as those purchased from breeders and fanciers, as taming requires the caregiver to personally dedicate time and attention to each animal. This may not be possible for a pet store owner to do on a daily basis. Lack of individual attention and personalized attention towards feeding and health care routines may also result in the painted turtle becoming stressed and falling ill before it reaches you.

Those painted turtles who are housed together in cramped quarters without sufficient space for basking or swimming also tend to hold on to their aggressive natures in order to survive. Constant fights with other companions may also lead to injuries, infections and possible deformities in the chelonians. If your selected painted turtle has had to compete with other tank mates for space and food for a continued period, it may be almost impossible to completely tame them. Terrapins who have been attained from such environments are rarely known to survive past the first few weeks, let alone become domesticated or form lasting bonds with their caregivers.

If the nearest pet store is located in another town or city, and chooses to ship the painted turtle to you, the conditions of the shipping container also decide how healthy your pet will be when it arrives at your doorstep. Unless you personally choose your turtle after making an informed decision, buying a painted turtle from a pet store may not always be the most sensible choice in the long-term.

When you visit the pet store to select your pet, it's best to have at least a basic idea of how to differentiate between a male and female painted turtle, as well as prepare a mental checklist of signs of a healthy painted turtle. While examining the painted turtles to select a suitable candidate, here are some probable instances at the pet store that should raise red flags and cause you to reconsider your purchase:

• The dealer cannot differentiate between a male and female painted turtle,

• The dealer has no knowledge of the age, shell-measurement, breed or legal requirements of painted turtle ownership,

• Many painted turtles have been housed together in the same quarters, making them cramped,

• The painted turtle has already begun to show signs of distress (lethargy, listless or restless behavior) at the store.

If you choose to have your painted turtle shipped or are making your purchase online, ensure that the pet store or online retailer has a return or money-back policy in place, in case you are unhappy with your pet. The above red flags also apply to painted turtles who are shipped to your premises. In addition, you should also be wary if:

● The shipping crates shown to you have no burrowing spaces,

● The dealer makes plans to ship the painted turtles during the daytime - despite the painted turtles being diurnal. Activity such as being transported across borders during their waking hours will prevent the painted turtles from falling asleep and cause stress, agitation, even illness.

3. Buying from a Breeder

They may not be as easy to find as pet stores and online retailers, but if you are keen on bringing home a healthy painted turtle, locating your nearest reputed painted turtle breeder might be a safer and wiser option. Breeders are people who raise painted turtles for sale and profit, often caring for more than one generation at a time.

Raising painted turtles to appeal to potential caregivers forms the livelihood of breeders; they, therefore, take great pain to provide the right kind of care to the chelonians - be it housing them in commodious aquatic settings, providing timely - and plenty - nutritious food, and ensuring that each Painted turtle receives individual medical attention. Breeders also house painted turtles in compatible groups, pairings and species, allowing you to pick up multiple exotics with greater chances of the painted turtles getting along in case of a community set-up. Those professionals who specialize in painted turtles will often also take an interest in raising other turtle breeds, such as Yellow-bellied slider turtles, Cumberland sliders, Boxed turtles, Snapping turtles and the like, to widen your options.

Due to the meticulous effort contributed towards raising healthy and viable painted turtles, the cost of purchasing a pet from a breeder may be a little higher than the rate offered by your neighbourhood pet store. What you will receive in exchange for this extra sum, however, is a painted turtle with superior breeding, a positive social character than wild counterparts and fairly good health. Breeders will also possess ample knowledge of the 4-inch law and other legalities, and will be able to precisely pinpoint each variety of painted turtles out to you. They will also have records of the date of birth, breed, vaccinations, necessary permits and possibly even heredity, to share with you.

Many breeders take a personal interest in their painted turtles and like to make certain that they end up in a safe and loving house that can promise lifelong care. They also have hands-on experience at caring for painted turtles, and are often good sources of information on pet care. Thorough professionals at their job, breeders will be able to properly advise on the individual personality oddities of each reptile, can help you find reputed food and housing resources, and can also refer you to a trusted exotic pet expert for healthcare.

Breeders, especially those raising such aggressive species as painted turtles, are always looking for potential caregivers for their exotics, and will place advertisements on such platforms as newspaper classifieds, community newsletters and message boards, or even on the Internet. While largely an honest and hardworking group of people, you may still come across the odd breeder whose concerns are more financial than emotional. They may not have set out in the effort to raise tame painted turtles, or may have ignored their health and well-being, but will still quote rates that most top-quality breeders charge. It is best to make a personal visit to the breeder if you can, before you make your purchase, in order to evaluate the quality of care provided to the painted turtles, as well as the trustworthiness of the seller.

4. Buying from previous owners

Fanciers are often confused with breeders since they are individuals who usually advertise painted turtles for sale from their homes. The main difference between fanciers and breeders, however, is that fanciers chance upon painted turtle babies when their own pets lay a clutch that they are not able to raise themselves upon hatching. Often an unexpected surprise to the owners, painted turtles attained from fanciers may only be of a certain variety or colour, limiting your choices.

Since fanciers are not professional breeders, they are often not required to possess any certification or licenses to confirm their status as sellers. This can make them challenging to locate; their information won't be found on community pet forums or with reputed veterinarians. If they do have a chelonian for sale, however, fanciers will advertise through local media, and can be contacted accordingly.

Rare though these pets may be, painted turtles attained from fanciers are likely to have a healthier nature than their store-bought and professionally-bred counterparts. These painted turtles are raised in a domestic environment, and are comfortable with human interaction from the start. These painted turtles also receive individual attention and care from their caregivers, making them more likely to form a bond with you. Fanciers can also be dependable sources of advice and point you towards the best veterinarian, food brands and housing options for your pets.

On the flip side, fanciers, being individual owners, may not always possess the legal authority to either raise hatchlings, or sell them under the prohibitions exercised by the 4-inch law. In addition, some fanciers may not want to sell you young painted turtles at all; instead, they may try to pass off ageing, unwanted adults as prospective pets. To avoid such misfortunes, it is best that you pay a personal visit to the fancier, and confirm their credibility with local exotic pet communities, if possible.

5.   Bringing home a wild painted turtle

In areas that form their natural range, painted turtles can easily be spotted at the edge of river bank areas, at private muddy clearings, and even in the gardens and backyards of many residential settlements. Depending on whether they were raised in the wild, or let out by previous owners from a captive state, the painted turtles may be governed by laws limiting their possession, ownership and dislocation from their habitat. If you chance upon a painted turtle in the wild, it is important to understand that it cannot be picked and tamed using the same methods employed for a stray dog or cat.

As exotic cold-blooded reptiles, painted turtles will not become domesticated upon early human contact. It takes weeks, even months of behavioural therapy from professionally-trained rehabbers to adapt painted turtles rescued from the wild into captivity. As an unprofessional caregiver, you may not have the resources or the tolerance to provide such exacting care.

Moving from the wild to a captive state will require the painted turtle to learn new scavenging, basking and cohabitation patterns, get used to an unfamiliar housing environment, and accept different behavior patterns from strangers not usually interacted within their natural history. Without necessary education on the matter, trying to rehabilitate a painted turtle on your own may turn quickly hectic, both for you and the animal.

Wild painted turtles may also be carriers of salmonella, especially if they are found with a shell length of less than 4 inches, as per United States Wildlife law, and may pass on the disease to humans during interaction. Furthermore, attaining a painted turtle from the wild is strictly prohibited by several states across the United States with ownership and possession banned in two, and is punishable by hefty fines. If found abandoned in the wild, painted turtles are either best left alone, or rushed to the nearest exotic pet centre for medical attention and rehabilitation. For the purposes of purchase, it is wise to stick with reputed and reliable sources as breeders, fanciers and adoption homes for displaced or abandoned pets and exotics - these will provide you with painted turtles who have had prior exposure to human contact and will be easy to tame and bond with.

6.   Considerations in the UK and USA

Even though painted turtles may be most easily available through local pet stores, if you do not wish to adopt your pet from a trusted adoption home, it is advisable to buy such exotic pets from more reputed sources like breeders. Whether you live in the United States or United Kingdom, breeders are often trusted more than any other source to sale possible owner pets who have been legally attained, tamed and vaccinated.

If you live in the United States, most breeders and fanciers will place advertisements for painted turtles for sale on such websites as Exotic Animals for Sale or Domestic Sale. In the United Kingdom, painted turtles for sale can be found on websites as Preloved and Pets4Homes.

7.   Initial Check-ups and Vaccinations

Regardless of the means through which you acquire your terrapins, it is vital that they receive medical attention before they are brought home. Depending on the care provided to your turtles before being handed over to you, you may need to verify that your pet has no rudimentary illnesses or infections.

As we now know, painted turtles may potentially be carriers of salmonella, apart from other viral infections. If brought home with the virus, casual contact with the pet may lead to salmonella spreading among your family members. A simple test at the veterinary office can help prevent long-term lethal effects among your loved ones.

Technically, captive painted turtles are less-likely carriers of salmonella than their wild counterparts. Developed countries like the United States and United Kingdom have managed to keep the spread of salmonella among under control through strict laws, veterinary practices and awareness programs, reducing the risk of your pet – or you – being affected.

To prevent any chance of bringing home a potential host for salmonella, however, ensure that you ask your breeder or fancier for the necessary health certificates proving that your turtle has been given a clean bill of health. This certification does not promise that your turtle will be salmonella-free throughout its lifetime, but will at least avoid illness from entering your house at the time of purchase.

Other sources such as pet store vendors may or may not have their painted turtles medically certified; the care provided to pets is usually determined by the dedication of the vendor towards selling healthy specimen. Terrapins acquired from pet stores may also have sustained injuries or contracted respiratory or eye infections that are not instantly visible. To avoid any such mishaps, it is best to schedule an appointment with a reputed exotic pet expert for an initial round of check-ups on the day that your purchase your Painted turtle.

8.   Electronically tagging your Turtle?

Curious and independent by nature, even the most domesticated painted turtle will want to explore its immediate environment, usually for food or a nesting spot for her eggs, and could easily become lost. Devices such as embedded microchips serve as tracking equipment to help return lost pets to their owners. In addition, the microchips can also record such information as the breed of the animal and administered medications, helping your veterinarian monitor your pet's care more efficiently.

Electronic tags are often suggested for such animals as dogs, cats, and those domestic breeds who have been raised for profit, such as poultry and livestock. However, electronic tagging is not restricted to certain species or purposes; it is, in fact, recommended among as many domesticated pets, whether conventional or exotic, as possible.

Not larger than a long grain of rice, an electronic microchip is available in different models and can easily be inserted by a veterinarian with a simple procedure, if you make this choice. With the site of injection varying depending on the species of animal, most turtles and tortoises often have their tag inserted in the hind left limb with some tissue glue used to seal the skin folds together. This procedure is also relatively painless, and will only slightly prick your turtle.

Most pet stores and breeders across the United States and United Kingdom have pets such as dogs and cats electronically tagged, but this decision may vary among exotic pet breeders and vendors. As with vaccinations, it is best to ask your breeder if your pet has been tagged, as ownership details on the microchip must then be switched under your name and address.

If your painted turtle has not been micro chipped, you can acquire these electronic tags through such websites as ID Tag, and Smartchip. Once embedded, your pet's details can be registered with such companies as PetKey and Pet Protect - most registration websites recognize all popular electronic tag brands, making the identification, monitoring and tracking of your turtle hassle-free and convenient.

Chapter 4: Housing your Painted Turtle

You need to create a proper ecosystem for your painted turtle to be housed. Remember that these creatures are not the regular warm blooded pets that we know of such as the dog or the cat. Additionally, being amphibians, they have a certain requirement when it comes to water, the type of land and even the light. Typically, a painted turtle will be found near creeks, ponds, lakes etc. the water needs to be fresh and should be maintained at a certain temperature. With painted turtles, water plays a very important role as these turtles even hibernate under water.

1. Housing your Painted Turtle

While fixing up the housing area for your turtles, you will have to first ascertain the size of the tank intended to house your pets. This is determined largely by the number of painted turtles you wish to house in one enclosure, along with their age and gender at the time of ownership. Optimally, you should aim to keep one pair of Painted terrapins per enclosure, preferably a male and female of similar sizes.

You will find that a tank with a volume of approximately 60 gallons, with about 25-30 gallons of filled water houses one adult painted turtle with ease. If a pair of adults is your initial purchase, or you intend to raise the hatchlings within the same tank, it will then need a volume of at least 20 gallons of filled water for an adult turtle, with an additional 10 gallons for every extra turtle in the tank.

If you still find yourself unsure of the adequate volume of the tank for your individual turtle, try this calculation trick adopted by several turtle owners and breeders: 10 gallons for every square inch of your terrapin's shell should guide you towards picking a tank with a capacity of up to 60 or 70 gallons for an adult painted turtle.

While conventional glass or acrylic aquariums are popular and trusted housing options for most chelonians, some alternatives can also be suitable, while also being economical as a purchase and in upkeep. Among the most commonly recommended housing options for painted turtles include:

1. **Containers:** Plastic stock tanks

Advantages: Relatively cheaper than glass aquarium. Suitable for indoor and outdoor housing. Built especially to store water; ideal aquatic setting for turtles. Opaque black/grey walls offer privacy. Will support lighting, heating, filters and other fixtures. Highly durable; will last longer than other housing options.

Disadvantages: Not as attractive as glass aquarium. Opaque walls offer no view of turtles within.

Ideal usage: Can be bought from farm supply stores. Should be covered with canopy, screen covering or similar roof to prevent escape and regulate lighting. If used as outdoor housing, can also support drainage features.

2. **Containers:** Plastic storage containers

Advantages: Considerably cheaper than an aquarium.
Opaque/translucent walls offer privacy. Lightweight, portable, durable
Can fit filters, heating lamps, other fixtures. Available in many shapes and sizes.

Disadvantages: Less attractive than a glass aquarium. Requires additional support when filled with water. May develop cracks leading to water seepage.

Ideal usage: Opt for darker toned containers; avoid bright colors. Provide support with wooden or PVC frames or braces. Regulate and monitor water and temperature. Opt for clamp-style lighting.

3. Containers: Preformed/Custom ponds

Advantages: Highly customizable housing option that allows for personalization. Ideal for outdoor housing. Relatively durable compared to glass aquariums. Relatively cheaper than glass aquariums. Built for water storage. Can house separate basking and nesting areas within same space. Can support heating, lighting, filtering fixtures.

Disadvantages: Requires more thought and labor to set up than other housing. Not ideal for indoor housing without adequate support.

Ideal usage: Best if used for outdoor housing at ground level. If housing indoors, incorporate pond liner around the edges.

2. Regulating Temperature

The optimum temperature settings within your turtle's housing zone determines the difference between your pet surviving and thriving. With a small optimum temperature margin that allows for such basic activities as swimming, foraging and even sex determination among chelonians, it becomes your duty to ensure their housing can provide this favorable setting in captivity.

In their natural setting, painted terrapins thrive in ambient temperatures of 75-80 F (24-27 C). With daily tasks split between their terrestrial and aquatic spaces, an aquatic temperature of 75-78 F (23-26 C) and a basking zone temperature of 90-95 F (32-35 C) will be ideal. If you are raising painted hatchlings, the temperature of the water will have to be regulated at 78-80 F (26-27 C) for the first 12 months.

In a captive setting, painted turtles have curiously been studied to thrive in warmer temperature settings. This could be an inherent preference for the slightly warmer climates that facilitate such responses as basking, feeding, swimming and mating. Lower temperatures, conversely, are preferred during the cooler hours of the night and the winter months – a time of brumation and relative inactivity. However, it is necessary that this regulated temperature setting be monitored with diligence, so as not to force your terrapins into a state of duress.

When exposed to excessive hours of heat for days at a time, painted turtles may become severely dehydrated. On the other hand, if exposed to windy, icy drafts from vents for long periods, your terrapins will lose their appetite, become listless and may even contract pneumonia. Temperature is best monitored with a separate thermometer attached to each zone within the enclosure so you can accurately regulate conditions within the aquatic and basking areas.

If you live in an area with a cooler climatic setting, and feel the necessity for additional heating within the enclosure, submersible water heaters are an ideal solution. When submerged in water, the heaters slowly raise the temperature in a manner not troubling to your pet. Moreover, they are small and portable enough that you can place install more than one heater within the tank at spots of your preference.

Painted turtles depend on the ambient moisture to provide them with hydration, making it your duty to keep the tank consistently filled with fresh water that is warm enough to generate some humidity. Adequate ventilation also contributes towards a healthy housing environment, with clean oxygen becoming a prerequisite against overheating and disease control within the tank. This can be achieved by covering the top of the tank with a wire mesh fitting.

3. Providing ideal Lighting and Water

Poikilothermic and diurnal by nature, painted turtles depend heavily on the heat and light from the sun's rays for such tasks as basking and switching in and out of brumation. An indoor tank may either not be ideal to receive consistent sunlight, or may also dehydrate the turtles if placed directly under the sun – making artificial lighting an important feature of your tank.

Most popular lighting solutions also give out some heat, raising the overall temperature within the housing. In a tank with regulated heating, any additional emitted heat may be harmful to your pets. This does not, however, mean that you force your turtles to become nocturnal. The absence of light does not allow basking, degrading the health of both, your turtles and any live plants within the tank. The best lighting options for such housing conditions are UVA and UVB lighting fixtures, preferably low-wattage (5 or 10 %) fluorescent tubes.

UVA lighting has been found to have positive psychological benefits among chelonians, while UVB lighting, even if derived from an artificial source, helps them absorb vitamin D3, essential for bone growth and maintenance. Additionally, UVB lighting does not flood the tank with harsh light, giving your turtles plenty of dark and quiet spots that promote privacy. Placed at an angle at corners of the tank, this lighting solution also helps segregate areas in your tank meant for basking and rest. Since your turtles will need at least 10 hours away from direct light in order to rest for the next day, ensure that your light settings are regulated in a way that encourages basking activities during the daytime.

Regardless of the proportion of a dry basking zone to water volume within your tank, ensure that it is as clean and fresh as possible. Most painted turtles adapt perfectly well to regular tap water, kept at room temperature and regulated at the right setting within the tank, provided the water is free of any traces of chlorine. Chlorine has been noted to have negative effects among these chelonians, no matter how small, and in combination with other chemicals in tap water, may become potentially illness-inducing for your pet.

Chelonian breeders and owners have noticed that fresh rainwater also seems to be well-suited for the tank, provided this water has not been stagnant before collection. Stagnant rainwater is a breeding hotspot for germs, bacteria and viruses, and is inadvisable as an addition to your controlled ecosystem. You may think to use distilled water, but this may also be an unwise option. Distilled water is usually over-treated to the point where it is stripped off essential minerals that the terrapins will need. Bottled spring water is an ideal choice, but is too laughably expensive an option to consider for most potential owners.

If it is difficult or inconvenient for you to provide rainwater for your tank, you can undertake a simple de-chlorination process by treating your water a water conditioning kit. These inexpensive products are easily available at most local pet stores and markets, and have been especially designed to draw out traces of chlorine, another related particle known as chloramine, as well as any heavy metals.

4. Furnishing the housing area

Starting with the base, you may first want to set up a substrate for your tank. Curiously, painted turtles are quite comfortable in a tank without a substrate – preferring a densely covered floor only for privacy in a crowded tank. The absence of a stony substrate also prevents such unnecessary incidents as choking on a small pebble.

If you want to allow this level of privacy and add an aesthetic appeal to the tank, however, a substrate that can withstand moisture for a few weeks without becoming too damp and infestation-friendly is ideal.

Fill up the floor with large, flat, smooth stones that provide cover for the turtles, as well as support for live plants that you may want to decorate the tank with. What should be avoided are small gravelly stones and jagged pebbles that can be ingested easily. Painted turtles are highly curious, and gravel, sharp jagged stones, etc. may become lodged in the chelonians throat or rupture your pet's digestive tract on the way out.

The most essential element in the tank apart from the right amount of water, is a platform or zone specifically reserved for basking. Painted turtles will require a significant portion of their waking hours to indulge in basking activities – the light and heat helps them regulate body temperature, while providing their systems with nourishing UVA and UVB rays. The only requisites for an adequate basking zone are that it be at a significant level above the water (to enable dry basking), and that it not be too close to the basking lamps or roof of the tank. Provided your soldier can comfortably climb onto the platform, a basking zone can either be constructed by a broad platform atop large flat stones stacked over each other in the corner of a tank, or can be purchased from your exotic pet store.

After the basics of the tank are taken care of, other elements should all be aimed towards providing exercise, as well as ensuring that the painted does not become stressed or listless. Your tank will please your pet if it contains some nooks, crannies and hiding spots in the water that do not obstruct its movements. Painteds love to hide and wander about areas with flat, broad bases; these spaces seem to bring them comfort during times of threat. They also add an ornamental beauty to your tank, making it a relaxing sight for your visitors and for you. Invest in such accessories as small logs, driftwood, flat large stones, small rocks etc. Remember that all items will need to be cleaned, washed and sterilized before depositing into the tank.

You can also fill the tank with some plants; while artificial plants are pleasing but merely decorative, live plants – provided they aren't toxic to the terrapins – are not just attractive, but also nourishing for your pets. Such aquatic flora as arrowheads, Common Eel Grass, Water Hyacinth, Canadian Pondweed, Hair Grass, Water Trumpet, Java Fern, Crystalwort, Java Moss and Water Lettuce.

5. Maintaining a hygienic housing environment

You may spend a fortune trying to set up an ideal habitat for your painted turtles, but, without dedicated time and the effort taken tp maintain a clean environment, you expose your pets to a host of infections and stress. A few simple measures, undertaken at regular intervals can help ensure your painted turtles thrive in a healthy setting:

1. A daily spot-cleaning of the tank is needed; through a mix of fecal waste and remains from live feed, painted turtles will find a way to dirty and decay the environment.

2. Water-filters should be detached from their spots and cleaned with plenty of water and a brush at least once a week, and disinfected once a month.

3. Temporarily house your turtles in a separate storage tub or tank while you carry out your cleaning duties – this simple act safeguards your pets against unnecessary ailments and infections from bacteria and allergens that coat a dirt and empty enclosure.

4. Old water must be flushed out, all accessories removed, washed, wiped and sterilized with a reptile-safe disinfectant before placing back into the tank.

5. All other fittings, such as, lighting, heating and filtration devices must be detached from their spots and cleaned, disinfecting those necessary.

6. Before you place your pets back into their tank, fill the tank with the requisite volume of fresh water, letting the water filter run one cycle as a precautionary measure against harmful aquatic infections.

7. If your tank has any elements making up the substrate, these, too, will have to be washed and disinfected with every cleaning. Try to replace old and withered gravel and pebbles as for flat, smooth ones as often as you can.

8. You will know a cleaning of your tank is long overdue when the water becomes overly cloudy and fecal and food particles float uninhibitedly around the tank. These floating materials are also indicative of a dirt filter that requires cleaning.

9. Ensure that you are especially careful while adjusting lighting, heat and temperature settings before placing you turtles back. Any irregularities in the housing conditions may trigger unnecessary physical and behavioral issues.

Chapter 5: What to Feed your Painted Turtle

Painted turtles are omnivorous creatures. While they will happily devour the commercially prepared pellet foods, they will also require live feed such as worms from time to time. You need to ensure that the feeding conditions are hygienic as even you are susceptible to infections from the foods eaten by these turtles. Regular cleaning is a must, especially after you have given your turtle live feed.

1.   Food Options

Natural Forage
Live feed

Though happy as adults with such vegetarian feed as plants and aquatic grasses, painted turtles are mainly omnivorous by nature means and will require a significant protein content that comes from meat – especially as growing hatchlings. Live feed such as small worms and insects are essential to help maintain healthy levels of calcium and phosphorus, especially in those areas with cooler climates. Live feed sources that easily accessible, easy to prepare and willingly accepted by the painted turtles include mealworms, earthworms, krill and crickets, sourced from pet stores in fresh or dried form. For aquatic feed, such options as tadpoles and different feeder fish breeds are most preferred. While live feed can be dropped into the tank, should you choose to provide the rare piece of cooked chicken or turkey, place them in dry feeding areas as food remains can contaminate the aquatic space almost immediately. It is best, however, to avoid option of providing such meats as beef and chicken as part of the turtles' nutrition, and provide tadpoles, feeder fish and worms – all safe options. All owners, agree, however, that raw mammalian meat is best avoided as part of your turtle's' diet under any circumstances.

Vegetables and Aquatic Plants

Painted turtles may not show the same enthusiasm towards all vegetables as they do for live feed and aquatic plants; these are however beneficial in nutritional value for a turtle raised in captivity and some should be added to their daily feeding schedule. Among the accepted vegetables are mustard and collard leaves, red and romaine lettuce leaves, bokchoy, kale, dandelion, carrots, beans and squash. Vegetables, if not the leafy kind, should preferably be chopped into bite-size cubes. Accepting a large portion of vegetables into their diet will often vary based on the age, personality and palate of each individual painted turtle, so it is best to try out a number of leafy green options with your pets to determine their taste. Aquatic plants as anacharis, duckweed, frog bit and water hyacinth in their daily diet also provides nutritional benefits. You can also introduce such produce as red lettuce and cabbage leaves provided sparingly. While your pets may develop a taste for lettuce and cabbages leaves, the chemical composition of these foods in excess can cause an upset stomach.

Fruits

Fruits are not always accepted with gusto among rehabilitated Painted turtles, largely since they are not easily found in their natural setting. If possible, avoid feeding your terrapin sugary and excessively fatty fruits, incorporating such rare treats in to their diet as grapes, blackberries, kiwis, pineapple pieces, strawberries, melon cubes and raspberries – all fruits with high vitamin profiles. Some fruits will need some chopping, peeling or de-seeding before feeding to the painted turtle, in order to avoid choking hazards or toxicity.

Bananas are best avoided, and if fed to the pets, should be peeled and chopped up before serving. Apples and oranges are highly favored, but will need to be de-pipped to avoid toxicity. Stones are best removed from such fruits as peaches, cherries, plums, nectarines and mangoes. The seeds of nectarines, avocados and mangoes, and the skin of avocados in particular, have been studied to be poisonous and cause toxicity in the turtles' systems.

2. Commercially Prepared Foods

As beneficial as live feed may be for the well-being of your turtle, in a captive environment and under your care, it works best as a supplement to your pet's diet. An artificial housing set-up may not have optimum foraging resources, and the turtle's greedy nature may prompt them to either eat excess fatty food or consume those items that may be toxic to their systems. Furthermore, painted turtles, based on their individual preferences and personalities may display a fussy attitude towards some vegetables and flora, healthy though they may be.

You can, therefore, take control of your terrapin's dietary needs by incorporating commercially prepared feed such as turtle pellets into mealtimes. Prepared to possess the necessary nutritional component for painted turtles in captivity, commercial feed is also considered essential for the optimum physical development of young ones.

To determine the brand best suited to your turtle, you can pick from such reputed brands as Purina AquaMax, Mazuri Freshwater Turtle Diet, Tetra ReptoMin, Nasco Turtle Brittle, Fluker's Aquatic Turtle Diet, HBH Turtle Bites and Nutrafin Turtle Gammarus.

If you have to feed freshly-hatched or turtles up to a year in age, you will have to include significant amounts of tissue-building protein. Ideally, protein forms about 60 percent of a growing painted turtle's diet, a majority of which can be provided through these commercial feeds. Past the age of one year, progress to foods that substitute excess protein for other essential nutrients such as calcium and phosphorus.

Most commercially pre-packaged turtle food can be purchased from your local pet stores. A common mistake that amateur owners make is to assume that the food manufactured for a certain aquatic species is suitable for all exotics in general. When purchasing feed for your painted turtle, ensure that is has been prepared for the type of aquatic you wish to raise - fish flakes, along with food for other semi-aquatic pets such as ducks are often manufactured with different nutritional compositions in mind, and are best avoided for your turtle. You can always contact your pet vendor, exotic chelonian expert or breeder for advice on the right type of feed for your painted turtle. Knowledgeable in the health and welfare needs of painted turtles, they can correctly guide you towards finding the right feed in your area.

3. The need for Calcium in Painted turtle feed

Painted turtles, too require significant amounts of calcium in their diet, both as developing hatchlings, and as adults for the maintenance of their carapace and bone structure. Adult painted females in particular, demand a significantly higher supply of calcium for better egg-laying along with shell-maintenance once they reach maturation.

Providing calcium in food, however, can be a complicated process as the intake needs to be carefully regulated. A deficiency of calcium in the diet will result in weaker shell structure and brittle eggs with poor hatchability among your females. Eggs that are laid may not hatch if the turtle's food has witnessed a deficiency in calcium content. An excess amount of calcium, on the other hand, is just as harmful and may result in egg-binding. You will, therefore, have to be careful towards the amount of calcium your turtles receive in comparison to such minerals as phosphorus or magnesium.

Those members in your tank who do not need large amounts of calcium will receive their supply of the mineral in commercially manufactured feed. For those painted turtles with a calcium deficiency, a mineral source can be provided within the tank for the pet to consume at their convenience.

A popular source of calcium preferred by many pet owners for reptiles is cuttlebone. Placed in a dry corner within the tank, your [ainted turtles will have easy access to this calcium source, should they feel lacking. Gut-loaded or calcium-dusted crickets also a preferred option and a favorite with the terrapins as well. Gut-loaded crickets will require some preparation through careful grinding, crushing and subsequent stuffing of calcium into the abdominal cavities of the crickets, but will make for a perfect calcium supplement.

Since calcium is an essential yet tricky mineral to navigate around, any doubts that you may have regarding its intake should be addressed with your chelonian pet expert. They will be able to correctly guide you and prevent any calcium-related mishaps from occurring within your tank.

2. What foods are acceptable for your Painted turtle?

LIVE FEED

1. Name: Crickets
   Dietary value: Dietary staple
   Frequency and preparation: Gut-loaded or dusted

2. Name: Earthworms
   Dietary value: Supplement to diet
   Frequency and preparation: Fresh, frozen, chopped

3. Name: Silkworms
   Dietary value: Supplement to diet
   Frequency and preparation: Fresh, frozen, chopped

4. Name: Waxworms
   Dietary value: Beneficial as rare treat
   Frequency and preparation: Fresh, frozen, chopped

5. Name: Mealworms
   Dietary value: Can be avoided
   Frequency and preparation: Fresh, frozen, chopped

6. Name: Superworms
   Dietary value: Can be avoided
   Frequency and preparation: Fresh, frozen, chopped

7. Name: Tubifex worms

Dietary value: Can be avoided
Frequency and preparation: Fresh, frozen, chopped

AQUATIC LIVE FEED

1. Name: Guppies
   Dietary value: Supplement to diet
   Frequency and preparation: Fresh, frozen, chopped

2. Name: Rosy-red minnows
   Dietary value: Supplement to diet
   Frequency and preparation: Fresh, frozen, chopped

3. Name: Daphnia
   Dietary value: Supplement to diet
   Frequency and preparation: Fresh, frozen, chopped

4. Name: Krill
   Dietary value: Beneficial as rare treat
   Frequency and preparation: Fresh, frozen, chopped, canned

5. Name: Shrimp(Gammarus)
   Dietary value: Beneficial as rare treat
   Frequency and preparation: Fresh, frozen, chopped, canned

6. Name: Tadpoles
   Dietary value: Beneficial as rare treat
   Frequency and preparation: Fresh, frozen, chopped

7. Name: Apple Snail
   Dietary value: Beneficial as rare treat
   Frequency and preparation: Fresh, frozen, chopped, canned

8. Name: Pond Snail
   Dietary value: Beneficial as rare treat

Frequency and preparation: Fresh, frozen, chopped, canned

9. Name: Mosquito larvae
   Dietary value: Beneficial as rare treat
   Frequency and preparation: Fresh, frozen, chopped

AQUATIC PLANTS

1. Name: Anacharis
   Dietary value: Essential in aquatic zone
   Frequency and preparation: Fresh, frozen, planted, hand-fed

2. Name: Duckweed
   Dietary value: Essential in aquatic zone
   Frequency and preparation: Fresh, frozen, planted, hand-fed

3. Name: Water Fern
   Dietary value: Essential in aquatic zone
   Frequency and preparation: Fresh, frozen, planted, hand-fed

4. Name: Water Hyacinth
   Dietary value: Essential in aquatic zone
   Frequency and preparation: Fresh, frozen, planted, hand-fed

5. Name: Water Lily
   Dietary value: Essential in aquatic zone
   Frequency and preparation: Fresh, frozen, planted, hand-fed

6. Name: Amazon Swords
   Dietary value: Beneficial as dietary staple
   Frequency and preparation: Fresh, frozen, planted, hand-fed

7. Name: Frogbit
   Dietary value: Beneficial as dietary staple
   Frequency and preparation: Fresh, frozen, planted, hand-fed

8. Name: Hornwort
   Dietary value: Beneficial as dietary staple
   Frequency and preparation: Fresh, frozen, planted, hand-fed

9. Name: Nasturtium
   Dietary value: Beneficial as dietary staple
   Frequency and preparation: Fresh, frozen, planted, hand-fed

10. Name: Pondweed
    Dietary value: Beneficial as dietary staple
    Frequency and preparation: Fresh, frozen, planted, hand-fed

11. Name: Water Lettuce
    Dietary value: Beneficial as dietary staple
    Frequency and preparation: Fresh, frozen, planted, hand-fed

12. Name: Water Milofil
    Dietary value: Beneficial as dietary staple
    Frequency and preparation: Fresh, frozen, planted, hand-fed

13. Name: Water Starwort
    Dietary value: Beneficial as dietary staple
    Frequency and preparation: Fresh, frozen, planted, hand-fed

VEGETABLES AND FRUITS

1. Name: Dandelion
   Dietary value: Essential dietary staple
   Frequency and preparation: Fresh, raw, chopped, whole

2. Name: Red leaf Lettuce
   Dietary value: Essential dietary staple
   Frequency and preparation: Fresh, raw, chopped

3. Name: Turnip leaves
   Dietary value: Essential dietary staple
   Frequency and preparation: Fresh, raw, chopped

4. Name: Collard greens
   Dietary value: Beneficial as rare treat
   Frequency and preparation: Fresh, raw, chopped

5. Name: Romaine lettuce
   Dietary value:
   Frequency and preparation: Fresh, raw, chopped

6. Name: Radicchio
   Dietary value: Beneficial as rare treat
   Frequency and preparation: Fresh, raw, chopped

7. Name: Carrots
   Dietary value: Part of staple diet
   Frequency and preparation: Fresh, raw, chopped

8. Name: Broccoli
   Dietary value: Can be avoided
   Frequency and preparation: Fresh, raw, chopped

9. Name: Cabbage
   Dietary value: Can be avoided
   Frequency and preparation: Fresh, raw, chopped

10. Name: Sweet Potato
    Dietary value: Part of staple diet
    Frequency and preparation: Fresh, raw, chopped

11. Name: Tomatoes
    Dietary value: Beneficial as rare treat
    Frequency and preparation: Fresh, raw, chopped

12. Name: Iceberg Lettuce
    Dietary value: Beneficial as rare treat
    Frequency and preparation: Fresh, raw, chopped

13. Name: Red pepper
    Dietary value: Beneficial as rare treat
    Frequency and preparation: Fresh, raw, chopped

14. Name: Endives
    Dietary value: Part of staple diet
    Frequency and preparation: Fresh, raw, chopped

15. Name: Kale
    Dietary value: Part of staple diet
    Frequency and preparation: Fresh, raw, chopped

16. Name: Green beans
    Dietary value: Part of staple diet
    Frequency and preparation: Fresh, raw, chopped

17. Name: Beets
    Dietary value: Can be avoided
    Frequency and preparation: Fresh, raw, chopped

18. Name: Sprouts
    Dietary value: Can be avoided
    Frequency and preparation: Fresh, raw, chopped

19. Name: Blueberries

Dietary value: Beneficial as rare treat
Frequency and preparation: Fresh, raw, chopped

20. Name: Blackberries
Dietary value: Beneficial as rare treat
Frequency and preparation: Fresh, raw, chopped

21. Name: Mango
Dietary value: Part of staple diet
Frequency and preparation: Fresh, raw, chopped, peeled

22. Name: Prickly pears
Dietary value: Part of staple diet
Frequency and preparation: Fresh, raw, chopped, de-stemmed

23. Name: Squash
Dietary value: Part of staple diet
Frequency and preparation: Fresh, raw, chopped, de-seeded, peeled

24. Name: Pumpkin
Dietary value: Part of staple diet
Frequency and preparation: Fresh, raw, chopped, de-seeded, peeled

25. Name: Watermelon
Dietary value: Beneficial as rare treat
Frequency and preparation: Fresh, raw, chopped, de-seeded, peeled

26. Name: Apple
Dietary value: Beneficial as rare treat
Frequency and preparation: Fresh, raw, chopped, de-seeded, peeled

27. Name: Papaya
Dietary value: Part of staple diet

Frequency and preparation: Fresh, raw, chopped, de-seeded, peeled

28. Name: Grapes
    Dietary value: Beneficial as rare treat
    Frequency and preparation: Fresh, raw, chopped, de-seeded, peeled

29. Name: Peach
    Dietary value: Beneficial as rare treat
    Frequency and preparation: Fresh, raw, chopped, de-seeded, peeled

30. Name: Cherries
    Dietary value: Beneficial as rare treat
    Frequency and preparation: Fresh, raw, chopped, de-seeded, peeled

31. Name: Plums
    Dietary value: Beneficial as rare treat
    Frequency and preparation: Fresh, raw, chopped, peeled

32. Name: Banana
    Dietary value: Beneficial as rare treat
    Frequency and preparation: Fresh, raw, chopped, peeled

33. Name: Cantaloupe
    Dietary value: Part of dietary staple
    Frequency and preparation: Fresh, raw, chopped,

34. Name: Strawberry
    Dietary value: Beneficial as rare treat
    Frequency and preparation: Fresh, raw, chopped,

COMMERCIAL PREPACKAGED TURTLE FEED

1. Name: Turtle Pellets
   Dietary value: Essential dietary staple

Frequency and preparation: 1 serving = size of turtle head (excluding neck)

2. Name: Processed worms
   Dietary value: Part of staple diet
   Frequency and preparation: Frozen, small serving

3. Name: Processed crickets
   Dietary value: Part of staple diet
   Frequency and preparation: Dried, frozen, gut-loaded

4. Name: Shrimp in brine
   Dietary value: Beneficial as rare treat
   Frequency and preparation: Feed as is

5. Name: Frozen feeder fish
   Dietary value: Part of staple diet
   Frequency and preparation: Feed as is

6. Name: Frozen shrimp
   Dietary value: Beneficial as rare treat
   Frequency and preparation: Feed as is

7. Name: Frozen krill
   Dietary value: Beneficial as rare treat
   Frequency and preparation: Feed as is

8. Name: De-shelled snails
   Dietary value: Can be avoided
   Frequency and preparation: Feed as is

MISCELLANEOUS FOOD ITEMS

1. Name: Canned fish (tuna, salmon)
Dietary value: Beneficial as rare treat
Frequency and preparation: Feed as is

2. Name: Chicken, turkey meat (cooked)

Dietary value: Can be avoided
Frequency and preparation: Cooked, chopped

3. Name: Eggs (boiled)
Dietary value: Can be avoided
Frequency and preparation: Cooked, chopped

3. Creating a healthy feeding habit

Painted turtles are creatures of summertime feeding and wintertime brumation while in their natural setting. Their appetites and the frequency of feed depends severely on the temperatures in their surroundings; while warmer climates will activate up their appetites, cooler temperatures brings about a loss of appetite. Therefore, you may find that you feed your painted terrapins with alarming frequency in the summer months, while the winters may require you to entice them with treats.

Hatchlings will need to be started with a carnivorous diet of live feed and commercial turtle pellets once each day. Requiring protein for their physical development, commercial pellets – with around 40 percent of your pet's daily protein intake – will make up half their daily feed, with the other half split between different live feed and the odd vegetarian or leafy food. Yearlings and adults, on the other hand, can be fed a largely herbivorous diet with commercial turtle pellets comprising 25 percent of the feed, and the rest split between plants, vegetables and some live feed for protein once every two days.

The frequency of your feed also matters in the upkeep of your enclosure; any extra food left to collect in the substrate will further contaminate the surroundings. As a rule of thumb, most painted turtle owners and breeders have found that the ideal portion of commercial feed per feeding is equal to the size of the turtle's head. Therefore, those painted terrapins with larger heads with get a bigger handful of pellets, while smaller turtles should ideally get a smaller portion. Do not underestimate the greedy disposition of the turtle, however; you can best determine how much each individual chelonian will need per feeding simply by watching how much it eats in one session.

On some occasions, monotony in the feed offered, lowered temperatures in the tank and other factors may lead to your painted turtle refusing food for prolonged periods. To entice your chelonians and activate their foraging behavior, you can use a piece of debris from the tank, such as a small twig or log instead of your fingers and hand tweezers, and place the food on it. Then, wave the debris close to the painted turtle, compelling it to chase after its feed. Should you be queasy about handling live feed, you can soak prepared feed in some tuna oil or brine to enhance its flavor and make it appetizing for the turtle.

Some owners prefer to move their pets to a separate environment for feeding and foraging. This setting is usually a stripped-down or replicated version of the main housing tank, built simply for feeding purposes. After they are done, the owners then transfer the pets back into their original setting. This practice is considered convenient for those who do not like to dirty the tank with leftover food debris and cause potential ailments among the pets.

Know, however, that it is not a necessary practice. While a steadfast precautionary measure against contamination and illness, you can also ensure the wellbeing of your pet by simply being disciplined in the upkeep and cleanliness of your tank. Furthermore, shifting the painted turtles from one tank to another constantly may agitate them, cause unnecessary stress and may even injure them in the process.

As long as you remember to clear away fecal matter and food debris a few hours after every feed, and filter and change the water on a regular basis, your environment should be healthy enough to house your terrapins for feeding as well as basking and rest. It is preferable that you feed the terrapins during the day, in order to complement their feeding routines in the wild. It is also essential that you maintain a regular frequency of enhancing your pets' feed with the necessary nutritional supplements.

4. Why the feed must be fresh

One factor that ensures the well-being of your pets and cannot be compromised is the freshness of your feed. Old or stale feed is susceptible to fungal growth and decay that may make your painted turtles very ill. Furthermore, mold can grow on just about any type of food - from the fresh produce you set aside as treats to commercially-prepared food packages.

The best way to ensure good-quality feed for your painted terrapins is to find reputed brands sold by reliable outlets and vendors, and stick with them. Before you pay for a bag of food, take the time to check if they are sealed closer to the date of production. If you find that the pellets are on sale and the price has been heavily discounted, pay close attention to the expiry date. Some vendors may try to deceive customers into buying older stock at throwaway prices to clear their shelves faster.

You may also be attracted to larger turtle pellet containers that seem economical and provide better "value for money". Before you succumb to this marketing tactic, understand that all types of food become open to moldy growth almost as soon as opened. Larger bags of food are a safer choice if you house a big group of turtles to care for, but may not be suitable for a single or pair of chelonians.

Favorable storage conditions also help to keep your feed fresh for longer. Most turtle pellets come in packages that may be a good short-term storage option, but if the feed is intended to last you a long time, empty the contents into airtight containers, preferably labeled with the expiry dates.

Every month or so, take stock of the feed you have stored aside. If expired food is harmful to your health, it is equally fatal for your Painted turtles. Do not feed them any food that has spoiled, collected mold or its past its shelf-life; any interaction with toxic substances can potentially endanger their lives.

5. Foods prohibited for your Painted turtle

Once you settle into a dietary pattern with your Painted chelonian, you may find that their appetites can be easy to fulfill; all they require is a constant supply of commercially-manufactured pellets to keep them appeased, supplemented by a small portion of plant life and some type of live feed. Such a hearty appetite may cause some to believe that these chelonians can be fed almost any type of food; this notion, however, is far from the truth. If you want to avoid health hazards among your tank members, ensure that your terrapins stay away from the following foods:

1.   Bread is not only a source of minimal nutrition to us, but also to painted turtles. Composed mainly of empty calories and sugar, these pets have a weakness for bread, and will ignore any nutritious food in its presence. Copious amounts of bread will fatten up your turtle without providing them with any useful nutrition. In their excitement, your pet may also try to swallow too much dry bread, which could lead to choking hazards.

2.   Many fruits may be too sugar-laden for your painted turtle on a daily basis, and cause digestive issues. Citric fruits such as oranges, lemons, grapefruit, and others like banana and apples are best fed as rare treats to your turtle.

3.   Other fresh produce that may be healthy for you but is incredibly toxic for chelonians includes leafy greens and produce with high oxalic acid, such as spinach. These foods may inhibit absorption of calcium by body, leading to Metabolic Bone Disease (MBD).

4.   Chocolate is also known to be highly toxic for painted turtles and can lead to poisoning, convulsions, nervous disorders, and death.

5.   Processed foods that are high in salts, sugar and unhealthy fats are just as bad for your pets as they are for you. While they may not be toxic for the pet, even tiny portions of processed foods may be too fatty for them.

6.   Fatty foods in general are best kept away from your painted turtle. Along with avocados and fatty processed foods, nuts should also be avoided. Along with filling your painted turtle with fatty content they don't require, nuts also may become trapped in the painted turtle's bills and choke them.

Chapter 6: Caring for your Painted Turtle

Unlike other pets, a pained turtle is not meant to be cuddled and fondled. In fact, when you handle a painted turtle too much, you will stress him out. Children who play with these turtles and tend to handle them too much will have to face nipping and scratching that is the turtle's reaction to stress. So when you are caring for your painted turtle, learning how to handle it is of primary importance.

1. Handling your painted turtle

It is essential, at the outset, to understand that painted turtles are not pets that can be cuddled or carried around in your pocket all day. As hatchlings, these turtles may be too delicate to handle for prolonged periods – and may be illegal in some parts to handle at all! As adults, many painted terrapins will likely discourage you from holding them beyond a few seconds or minutes. You may wisely choose to give your chelonian their personal space and avoid handling them altogether, but certain situations will call for you to lift, grasp and even examine the reptiles for maladies and wounds.

Careful and cautious though you may be, you may still find it a challenge to successfully handle your painted terrapin - don't, however, be dismayed. Painted turtles are smaller in size than their red-eared slider cousins, slippery to touch, yet surprisingly agile and strong reptiles who take great pride in their defensetactics. In such situations, it is smart to be calm yet firm in your approach, grasp and interaction with your pet. Any abrupt movements, sudden noise or a large group of people rushing towards the turtle may agitate it and cause it to react defensively, by hissing, scratching, swimming rapidly away or even emptying the contents of their cloaca. The best tried-and-tested time to handle your pet is to approach it in stealth when it is basking.

71

Lifting your painted turtle

Once you do approach your painted turtle, lifting it correctly is of utmost importance. Remember, an adult painted turtle may be slightly temperamental, so its defense tactics are likely to be painful to the recipient. Another point to remember is that the painted turtle cannot, and should not be lifted in the same casual manner that other domestic animals such as dogs or cats are. Do not try to pick them by their feet with their mouth facing your face or body – they may either injure you, or you may cause them severe injury, possibly even a fracture.

The best way to lift your painted turtle is to place one hand each on its carapace and beneath its plastron in a calm and slow motion. When you lift the reptile, support its feet with your palm by placing a hand beneath its feet to prevent it from kicking at you either in fight or fright. As your pet has sharply-tipped claws, your grasp prevents the chelonian from clawing at you with its nails.

Once you have finished examining your turtle, place it back down within the tank on its basking platform in one smooth motion. Avoid releasing your pet into the water, as it may not be ready to swim and may struggle. Understand that most domesticated turtles in general, and some individual painted turtles, in particular, may not want to be handled unless absolutely necessary; too much pressure may not only stress them, but also cause damages to their physical frame.

Interacting with Painted turtles and the risk of Salmonella

Since the risk of exposure to salmonella from Painted turtles is both, easily possible and preventable, smart sanitary precautions, safe handling techniques, and an awareness of hygiene around exotic pets can go a long way in preventing its spread in your household. In cramped spaces that house several species of pets together, Painted turtles are best kept separate from such ready transmitters of bacterial parasites as chickens.

When handling your terrapins, designate a pair of clothing and shoes specifically for interaction with them. Ensure that these items are cleaned and disinfected and stored away from other personal items after handling your pets. Avoid letting your turtles loose in such easily contaminated areas as the kitchen, bathroom or any room that contains food, clothing or objects reserved for human use.

Remember to wash your hands and face with antibacterial soaps after each visit to the tank, and supervise younger children and amateur handlers during their cleaning procedures. Ensure that such tasks as handling, feeding, cleaning and egg hatching are either carried out by you, or a person specifically entrusted with the responsibility; exposing the turtle to several humans at once – especially children - increases the risk of infection among all involved parties.

Finally, be proactive at educating children and other adults about the right methods to interact with and care for painted turtles – awareness and proper education, after all, is key to a healthy painted turtle, and a healthy you.

2. Transporting your painted turtle

Happy though they may be within their aquatic housing zones, you will face certain situations during which you may have to transport your painted turtles out of their enclosures. These may include medical visits to the veterinary office, trips to the local county fair or even longer journeys that may require boarding an airplane. Whatever be your need, transporting your pet in a manner that ensures comfort and adheres to necessary laws, is an issue of importance. Painted turtles may feel harassed in a moving vehicle with improper lighting and safety conditions, causing stress both, to themselves and to you. To safely cart around your terrapins, among the most preferred storage containers are opaque plastic storage tubs with lids.

Plastic storage containers are the easiest and most economical means through which you can transport your chelonian friends around. All your tub needs is a firm roof that prevents the pet from climbing out when startled. Some smartly placed holes drilled into the top of the top for ventilation and a means to allow air flow in the tub and a pile of newspapers to absorb waste material produced by your pet should complete your preparation. Remember that painted turtles should never be transported in an aquatic setting – water in a moving vehicle may cause unnecessary mishaps, injuries, even drowning.

The only factor to consider regarding your pet's safety is that your painted turtle should be as stress-free as possible. Mostly caused by abrupt changes in scenery or excessive handling, stressors can be avoided by choosing translucent transportation tubs for your pets. These will shield your turtles from constantly changing scenery, while the lighter colors and environment will let in some light and allow basking behavior. Transparent plastic tubs are also a good option to help encourage basking, but may stress your turtle owing to the lack of protective barrier from the changing scenery outside.

It is also essential that you regulate the temperature within the box in order to keep your turtle as calm as possible. A comfortable setting between 75-80 degrees Fahrenheit should help keep your painted turtle at its calmest.

Tips to ensure safe painted turtle transportation

1. Secure your tub to your car to prevent it from sliding around and injuring your turtle. You can do this by buckling the seat belt around the container, or use some bungee cords. This will ensure that your painted turtle is not thrown around the vehicle in case of turbulence.

2. If the temperatures in your area fall below the recommended 75 degrees Fahrenheit for painted turtles, you can keep them warm with a hot-water bottle. Wrapped in a towel and fastened to the top inner corner of the container, this simple measure will keep your turtles warm during transportation.

3. If the temperatures in your surroundings exceed the recommended 80 degrees Fahrenheit for your turtles, you can cool your pet using a water spray or cool cloth. In case of excessively high temperatures in your car, place the container away from

direct sunlight, and try to adjust the temperature with your air-conditioner.

4. It is best not to transport your turtle with a large group of passengers, as a large group within a cramped space alters the temperatures, noise and oxygen levels within the vehicle. Loud music and other disturbing behavior may also cause duress, making the cargo section your ideal solution.

5. If you are traveling overseas with your painted turtle and need to board an airplane, contact your airline to learn the necessary transportation, electronic tagging and medical preparations that need to be undertaken.

6. Remember to verify and complete such air transport procedures as filing the necessary paperwork, giving your pet the necessary vaccinations and clearances, and securing permits for on-board carriage.

7. Finally, assure that all your travelling companions – whether your fellow car passengers, or crew on-board your airline – are aware of the presence of your turtle and are comfortable with having it travel with them.

3. Caring for your painted turtle in the winter

The winter months are both, a critical as well as relaxing time in the life cycle of a painted turtle, whether in captivity or in the wild. In their natural surroundings, most painted terrapins survive the harsh winter season by entering a state of partial hibernation – known as brumation – while floating safely at the depth of such freshwater bodies as ponds. It is the thick yet soft vegetative flooring at the bottom, along with the padded muddy embankments that provide Painted turtles with the necessary cover needed to survive the months.

During this brumative period, painted turtles undergo very low levels of activity with their metabolism dropping by almost 90 percent. This is largely caused by the lower consumption, yet higher burning rate of oxygen at colder temperatures. This partial shutdown is also helped by the painted turtle's ability to absorb oxygen from its surroundings through the membranes around its throat, mouth and even cloaca. While using up the glycogen content stored in its body for nutrition. Mostly undertaken in order to survive the bitter chill in most North American states, this state of torpor pauses such daily activities as basking, feeding and even swimming, until the conditions above water reach a more favorable temperature of around 60 degrees Fahrenheit.

In theory, to help your painted turtles survive the winter months, brumation should ideally be undertaken, particularly if you live in areas that experience bitter winters with water that freezes over (such as parts of the United States and Canada). Through the introduction of this species to a variety of geographical and climatic conditions over the years, however, it has been found that painted turtles can actually spend the winter months without needing to brumate, if given the right ambient and aquatic settings. With the choice to partake in an intricately complicated phenomenon, a painted turtle that does enter a state of brumation in captivity may not always find conditions favorable enough to emerge from its state in complete health. Furthermore, the aquatic set-up provided in captivity may not have the depth, surface area or even vegetative cover necessary for successful brumation. Irregularities and constant shifts in the water temperature may cause the turtles to enter a state of shock, unbeknownst to you. A difficulty on your part to maintain the right temperature of the water at all times could also shut down your pet's anatomy entirely, instead of lulling it into seasonal sleep.

Whether your painted turtles are housed outdoors or raised within your home also impacts their personal decision to enter a brumative state. You will also need to check on your pet every few days, without abruptly breaking their state of torpor. Any deviation from this routine may only serve to traumatize your pet through the winter months instead of helping it thrive. It is never easy for herpetological experts, let alone amateur caregivers, to accurately isolate the factors that successfully take painted turtles in and out of their brumative cycle. As an amateur pet owner, you may have a basic knowledge of the ideal water, temperature and lighting settings for effective brumation, but unless you can consistently replicate the painted turtles' natural habitat for the entirety of winter, and have sufficient experience in doing so, avoiding your terrapins from entering the brumative state during the winter is the best course of action.

As a caregiver, therefore, you will have to assess whether you are ready to encourage brumation in your turtles. If yes, you will then need to determine if your housing set-up can protect your painted turtles against the extremities that winter in your area may bring. Regardless of their geographical location and the care they can provide, many professional painted turtle breeders and owners most often choose to discourage brumation and keep their turtles active in the winter.

Setting the tank up for winter

An outdoor housing enclosure may expose the painted terrapins to chilly drafts of wind during the winter months, and must ideally be switched for indoor housing. If you are unable to move your painted terrapins indoors due to lack of space or preparation time, you will then need to enclose your chelonian housing zone within a wind-proof insulated cover layer. It's best to work ahead of the winter by designating a brumation zone in a room on your premises - such as an empty bedroom, tool shed or garage - that will be undisturbed by other members in your family.

For a warm aquatic setting that keeps your turtles active, set the water temperature between 75 and 78 F (24-26 C), ensuring that it does not abruptly fall below accepted levels. In the wild, painted turtles nourish themselves in winter months by avoiding foraging behavior, choosing instead to use up their glycogen reserves, just as mammals use stored fat during hibernation. In captivity, you will continue to feed them as per your regular schedule, taking special care to monitor your pet's appetite. Water that is too cold may shut down hunger responses in the turtles, and encourage the production of lactic acid as part of their anaerobic functions – highly undesirable if you want to keep your painted turtles out of brumation. Without sufficient levels of magnesium and calcium to neutralize the lactic acid, accompanied by the right water and ambient setting, poor feeding habits during the winter months may also spell doom for your painted turtle.

You may also have fewer hours of natural light in an indoor enclosure during the winter, so ensure that the necessary UVA and UVB lighting arrangements have been made to maintain daily basking activities at the stipulated hours. Few other causal factors can shut a painted turtle's body down faster than inadequate heat and light; regulate a steady minimum of 12 hours of light each day to help keep your pets active and out of the tricky brumation zone.

4. Locating your missing Painted Turtle

1. Situation: Turtles lost within the house

Immediate actions: Lock up all doors, windows, gates, limit family members, pets to one room, check all rooms, doorways, under surfaces, check different floors within house, check nooks, crannies, corners, listen for faint scratching sound of claws against hard floors/walls.

Long-term action: Determine 1-2 week survival period in the wild, set out bowl with water/food for turtle to find, spend daytime hours searching for pet instead of night.

Preventive measures: Set up better lids/screens for tank or housing enclosure, set up preventive barriers at entry/exit of the house, restrict free-range roaming, invest in electronic tagging.

2. Situation: Turtles lost outside the house

Immediate actions: Lock up all doors, windows, gates, limit family members/ pets to one room, check all rooms, doorways, adjoining interiors, check areas that provide cover such as bushes/muddy banks, check outdoor nooks/crannies/corners, follow direction of local stream/pond or freshwater body if present nearby, inspect community water bodies for potential basking zones, listen for scratching sounds in
areas with leafy, wood floor cover.

Long-term action: Determine 1-2 week survival period in the wild, set out bowl with water/food for turtle to find, spend daytime hours searching for pet instead of night, enlist help of friends, family, local police/vet /office/social media.

Preventive measures: Set up better lids, screens for tank or housing enclosure, set up preventive barriers at entry/exit of the property, restrict free-range roaming, invest in electronic tagging, invest in such security measures as guard dog/electronic alarms.

3. **Situation:** Lost and found turtle

Immediate actions: Inspect shell/limbs, skin for injury, cuts, wounds, abscess, physical trauma, inspect bones and shell for fracture or bleeding, check eyes, ears, appetite, soak turtle in bowl of lukewarm water to clean away dirt/dust, resume feeding as per normal/resist overfeeding.

Long-term action: Refer to veterinary hospital in case of any visible trauma symptoms, isolate pet from other tank mates during the recovery period, conduct round of laboratory tests to check for other possible ailments/injuries, provide hydration by soaking turtle in Pedialyte solution as per instructions.

Preventive measures: Set up better lids/screens for tank or housing enclosure, set up preventive barriers at entry/exit of the property, restrict free- range roaming, invest in electronic tagging, invest in such security measures as guard dog/electronic alarms.

5. Entrusting others with your Painted turtle

1. **Type of care: Possible caregiver**

Short-term care in your absence (under 48 hrs): Family member, friend, neighbor.

Long-term care in your absence (over 48 hrs.): Family member, friend, neighbor, house sitter.

Temporary care by another person: Family member, friend, neighbor, veterinary services.

Re-homing Painted Turtles: Family member, friend, neighbors, hobbyists, rescue centers, breeders.

2. **Type of care: Food**

Short-term care in your absence (under 48 hrs): Will last up to 48 hours without needing another feed (adult), provide instructions on live feed, vegetation, harmful foods, provide commercial feed to caregiver (if needed).

Long-term care in your absence (over 48 hrs.): Add aquatic plants or feeder fish to sustain hunger, provide commercial feed to caregiver, provide instructions on live feed, vegetation, harmful foods.

Temporary care by another person: Add aquatic plants/feeder fish to sustain hunger, provide commercial feed to caregiver, provide instructions on live feed, vegetation, harmful foods.

Re-homing painted Turtles: Provide/recommend preferred commercial feed and aquatic vegetation to caregiver, provide instructions on live feed, vegetation, harmful foods.

3. Type of care: Lighting

Short-term care in your absence (under 48 hrs): Set lighting periods with timer in system, instruct caregiver to monitor lights/basking.

Long-term care in your absence (over 48 hrs.): Set lighting periods with timer in system, instruct caregiver to monitor lights/basking every 2-3 days.

Temporary care by another person: Set lighting periods with timer in system, instruct caregiver to monitor lights/basking every 2-3 days, provide replacement UVA/UVB bulbs.

Re-homing Painted Turtles: Recommend preferred lighting periods, instruct caregiver to monitor lights/basking every 2-3 days, recommend preferred UVA/UVB bulbs.

4. Type of care: Heat

Short-term care in your absence (under 48 hrs): Set predetermined regulated temperature with timer, provide instructions on adjusting temperature, instruct caregiver to monitor temperature.

Long-term care in your absence (over 48 hrs.): Set predetermined regulated temperature with timer, provide instructions on adjusting temperature, instruct caregiver to monitor temperature.

Temporary care by another person: Set predetermined regulated temperature with timer, provide instructions on adjusting temperature, instruct caregiver to monitor temperature, provide replacement heating lamps, thermometers.

Re-homing Painted Turtles: Provide instructions, suggestions on proper temperature/heat/basking conditions, recommend preferred temperatures to caregiver, provide/suggest preferred heating lamps/thermometers.

5. Type of care: Water

Short-term care in your absence (under 48 hrs): Filter once daily, maintain regulated temperature.

Long-term care in your absence (over 48 hrs.): Filter once daily, collect debris every 2 days, maintain regulated temperature.

Temporary care by another person: Filter once daily, collect debris every 2 days, change water every 30 days, disinfect and condition water, maintain regulated temperature.

Re-homing Painted Turtles: Provide instructions,suggestions on proper water conditions, recommend preferred water filters.

6. Type of care: Health/Safety

Short-term care in your absence (under 48 hrs): Ensure that turtle displays signs of health, predator-and-escape- proof surroundings, provide handling instructions.

Long-term care in your absence (over 48 hrs.): Provide first-aid medication, pet expert contacts, instruct on basic first-aid, provide care sheet, predator-and-escape-proof surroundings, provide handling instructions.

Temporary care by another person: Provide handling instructions, provide first aid medication, pet expert contacts, instruct on basic first-aid, provide care sheet, recommend predator-and-escape-proofing surroundings.

Re-homing Painted Turtles: Provide/recommend first-aid medication, pet expert contacts, instruct on basic first-aid, provide care sheet, recommend predator-and- escape-proofing surroundings, provide handling instructions.

Chapter 7: Health concerns for your Painted Turtle

Painted turtles are among the hardier of the reptilian creatures and have immune systems that can withstand illnesses and infection of a varying nature. Their health, however, is not infallible, and is susceptible to a host of ailments if housed in unfavorable conditions. Furthermore, most health-related ailments in painted turtle turtles are of a nature that can only be isolated and diagnosed through laboratory examinations.

If provided with the right care, timely check-ups and a hygienic housing environment, most painted turtles will live their days in robust health, only affected in their old age by such ailments as shell-related decay or injuries, organ failure or drowning. Most common infections and physical ailment caused in these terrapins can be traced to an imbalance in their diet, poor housing conditions or external psychological factors that indirectly impact their emotional well-being.

A healthy painted turtle is alert even while it is basking or resting, and engages in a constant stream of activity such as swimming, foraging, nest-preparing (for females during the reproductive season) or basking throughout its waking hours. Painted turtles with no signs of infection or illness will display such signs of health as clear eyes, with no discharge (either colored or smelly) oozing from their nose or ears. A smooth-to-touch carapace with even, distinct and vibrant coloring and without any patchy white growth, pinkish-red hue or foul odor are other signs of a healthy painted turtle; a shell with cracks, injured or misaligned limbs, closed or swollen eyes and bloody discharge either from the shell or cloaca regions are often indicators of a more severe physical condition. Generally robust during the diurnal hours, any displays of prolonged lethargic or listless behavior by your painted turtle should cause concern, especially if accompanied by physical indicators of ill health.

At the first display of an illness-related symptom, your immediate course of action to should be to ensure that your painted turtle is in no immediate danger of drowning or dehydration. As a precautionary measure, try first to raise the water temperature of the tank (already set to 75 degrees Fahrenheit) by about 5 or 10 degrees Fahrenheit. Cold-blooded by nature, painted turtles are unable to regulate their body temperatures to match the outer conditions, and a warmer setting should help your pet's body temperature rise enough to activate necessary physiological functions; most symptoms of listlessness or lethargy can be dealt with in this manner. Should this first-aid step make no difference to the health of your pet, or further aggravate its illness, rush your painted turtle to your exotic pet expert for an immediate diagnosis and treatment plan.

If afflicted by a grave health condition past the initial stage of medication, most painted turtles, despite their general hardy disposition, may be too far removed from their natural habitat and conditions to withstand the trauma that accompanies any disease or injury. As a rule of thumb, such a distressing environment within your vivarium can be avoided simply by ensuring that you are committed to providing hygienic housing and feeding standards that keep sickness at bay.

1. Common infections and maladies

Metabolic Bone Disease

Metabolic Bone Disease is a common deficiency-related illness that is mostly seen among those painted turtles in the development or adult stage who are given inadequate levels of calcium and disproportionately large amounts of phosphorus in their feed. If left unchecked, Metabolic Bone Disease, also known as MBD, will result in the eventual weakening of bones, become an underlying cause for other illnesses, and may even cause untimely death.

Less than ideal proportions in calcium and phosphorus intake generally occurs when your painted turtle's diet is rich in phosphorus, but not in calcium. A low supply of vitamin D3 – derived largely from UVB rays – and necessary for the absorption of calcium from food sources, may also be a significant causal factor. If housed indoors with improper lighting arrangements and inadequate basking facilities, painted turtles are forced to rely solely on food for their daily supply of this vitamin. If Vitamin D3 provided in tiny quantities, the turtle's system may be unable to break down and absorb the calcium it needs, even if it is supplied in plenty in its food. Food rich in oxalic acids such as spinach and chocolate may further obstruct the absorption of calcium, further weakening your pet's bone structure.

Once stricken, the symptoms and subsequent effects of MBD can take weeks, even months of medication and rehabilitation to nullify, making its prevention a higher priority than its cure. Initial symptoms include prolonged durations of drowsiness and lethargy, decreased levels of activity with little or no swimming, basking, or walking, a shaky gait and movement, loss of appetite, visible frailty in bone structure, a deformed or irregular physical appearance, probable seizure episodes, and partial or total abrupt paralysis. Terrapins afflicted with MBD may also have a shell that feels cold no matter what time of day - this is because MBD disrupts the animal's ability to regulate body temperature, furthering weakening its health.

You may also find that it takes longer than usual to raise your reptile's body temperature, and that such efforts may be physically strenuous for the pet. It is for this reason that painted turtles should be given veterinary care as soon as any symptoms of MBD are exhibited. Based on the severity of the illness, most pet experts will advise a prolonged treatment with a calcium supplement such as Rep Cal. If your painted turtle has already suffered a seizure episode and is close to physical collapse or death, its veterinarian may even provide an intravenous dose of liquid calcium to the animal, to help sustain therapy and treatment.

All prescribed calcium supplements will have to be added to each feed in the recommended doses; the turtle will also have to be isolated from its companions and kept in highly regulated and monitored conditions. Heating and lighting fixtures will need to be adjusted to the terrapin's changing needs to promote quicker recovery.

Despite early signs of recovery, those terrapins who have suffered seizures while overcome with MBD may still experience an episode once a week or less in the coming few months. It is best to monitor your pet's road to recovery under the supervision of its veterinarian, to help guarantee that the chelonian is receiving the best level of care possible. If given the right kind of rehabilitation, painted turtles can make a recovery from MBD in a span of six to eight weeks, or even less.

Respiratory Infections

Respiratory Infections (RIs) are not only fatal for a painted terrapin's health, but are also of a highly contagious nature, and will likely befall other chelonians housed within the same enclosure. Not caused simply by a concentrated or specific strain of virus, RIs can take seed from the turtle being exposed to an array of unhealthy housing factors, ranging from unhygienic and unfiltered water to an abrupt and prolonged exposure to cold drafts from outside the aquarium, from an accumulation of food, mold and fecal debris in the substrate, to an infection contracted from another ill tank mate.

If afflicted, painted turtles will exhibit such symptoms of respiratory infections as severe difficulty while breathing, along with by peculiar motor movements, collectively known as listing. Listing is best explained as a pattern of swimming motor activities that look nothing like a healthy turtle's usual swimming movements. Clearly visible through such acts as imbalanced motor function, unsteady maneuvering of the water and even swimming in circles, these erratic activities are the result of a build-up of fluid in the terrapin's lungs. This fluid, when accompanied by irregular breathing and listing, is often indicative of a larger infection in your turtle's system, possibly even pneumonia. Other symptoms displayed by a painted turtle overcome with any RI include the following instances:

Respiratory condition: Wheezing sounds while breathing
Nature of occurrence: During periods of high activity, observed in overweight turtles.
Visible red flags: Prolonged wheezing, with audible difficulty in breathing.

Respiratory condition: Open mouth while breathing
Nature of occurrence: Commonly observed during basking
Visible red flags: Prolonged open mouth, accompanied by wheezing sounds and discharge of mucus.

Respiratory condition: Sneezing

Nature of occurrence: Generally observed while underwater

Visible red flags: Prolonged sneezing in and out of water, accompanied by discharge of mucus, open mouth, wheezing, coughing and general listless behavior.

Respiratory condition: Coughing (with or without vomit)
Nature of occurrence: During feeding or upon superficial irritation to respiratory or digestive system.

Visible red flags: Prolonged regular coughing/vomiting, choking sounds, visual indicators of mouth rot.

Respiratory condition: Yawning
Nature of occurrence: Commonly observed during basking or while underwater
Visible red flags: Prolonged yawning, accompanied by wheezing sounds, open mouth, lethargy and discharge of mucus

Respiratory condition: Appearance of bubbles from nose and mouth
Nature of occurrence: Commonly observed while underwater
Visible red flags: Prolonged appearance of bubbles/foamy discharge while outside water.

As RIs are often brought on by inhospitable conditions in the housing environment, there is little by way of medication that can help treat your pet. A veterinarian may be able to help ease discomfort and restore some health in the reptile by administering a treatment with an effective antibiotic known as Baytril. As many other exotic pets, painted turtles often respond both quickly and positively to Baytril, and will appear to have made a recovery almost overnight – understand, however, that the treatment will still have to be followed adhering to the veterinarian's orders, to prevent a possible relapse.

Those painted turtles who have incurred an RI will also have to be isolated from their tank-mates, and should only rejoin their companions when their recovery is complete and their original housing conditions have been attended to. If the cause for the infection is a factor within the tank such as unchanged water, an unclean substrate or poor heating and lighting, all pets from the tank will also have to be shifted while the housing is disinfected and the contents changed. On your part, any clothing worn during the disinfection task must either be cleaned separately from other laundry, or disposed of entirely. Painted turtles may not be able to pass on a cold to you, but the viral strains from their infections can be transmitted to other susceptible animals through media such as clothing.

2. Shell-related issues

Ailment: Algae growth

Symptoms: Pale green patches of algae growth appearing at sporadic intervals on the scutes.

Probable cause: Mostly observed in outdoor aquatic housing facilities and wild Painted turtles, not hazardous to health in small quantities.

Treatment: Gentle wiping of shell with soft moist cloth or soft-bristled toothbrush and water, filtration of water.

Ailment: Cracks/Shell-damage

Symptoms: Crack or hole in the scute, missing scute, foul smell, bleeding, infection, shock.

Probable cause: Injury, attack, underlying infection or shell rot, with long-term exposure and neglected treatment leading to organ failure, disability, even death.

Treatment: First-aid in case of superficial shell damage; immediate medical attention in case of severe or persistent damage.

Ailment: Discoloration

Symptoms: Light or whitish patches on shell surface, golden appearance of certain scutes.

Probable cause: Bacterial or fungal infection, mineral deposits or scutes shedding.

Treatment: Move turtle into sanitary conditions, monitor diet, water and filtration procedures, refer to pet expert in case of persistent discoloration.

Ailment: Unnatural coloring

Symptoms: Pink to red coloring around scutes, carapace, plastron, skin.

Probable cause: Blood poisoning (septicemia), caused due to previous injury, illness, unsanitary conditions.

Treatment: Refer turtle to exotic pet veterinarian immediately

Ailment: Fungal growth
Symptoms: White to brown fuzzy clumps of growth on shell surface.
Probable cause: Insufficient filtration of water, inadequate basking requirements, contracted from other infected turtles.
Treatment: Administer Repti Turtle Sulfa Dip for mild cases and external infections; report persistent cases to veterinarian

Ailment: Mineral deposit
Symptoms: Collection of white, chalky calcium and magnesium deposits on shell surface.
Probable cause: Long-term exposure to hard water, while not hazardous to health, may affect structure and health of shell
Treatment: Use filtered and purified water, preferably also de-chlorinated.

Ailment: Pyramid syndrome
Symptoms: Rough appearance of shell, "pyramid" formations of scutes, uneven shell surface.
Probable cause: Excess intake of fats and protein, leading to accelerated scute growth and uneven "pyramid" appearance, long-term exposure can lead to kidney failure and damaged shell.
Treatment: Reduce protein intake in food, monitor feeding, avoid overfeeding.

Painted turtles and the Scute Shedding Phenomenon

The scutes on a painted turtle's carapace possess a nature highly similar to the hair on human skin, the fur on mammalian bodies, or even the scales found on such reptiles as Tiger Salamanders. Appendages that are mostly composed of a protein compound known as keratin, scutes are inherently non-living components of the dermis and extend outward from the turtle's body as a means of protection and adornment, with the oldest scutes found on the outermost parts of the shell, and newer ones making their appearance in the inner regions.

In tandem with the cycle of growth, shedding and re-emergence, the scutes on a painted turtle's carapace shed at regular intervals to make way for newer, healthier scutes which are more resistant to the harsh factors posed by the external environment. As old scutes separate and break away from the shell, tiny parcels of air becomes nestled between the shell surface and skin, lending the carapace a golden hue. Through a gentle yet persistent detachment from the skin, the light-hued scutes eventually break away from the turtle's body, allowing for smoother, healthier scutes to emerge from underneath.

This shedding period among painted turtles, however, may not always be a subtle and invisible process; it may, in fact, be almost alarming to the uninformed eye or a new exotic pet owner. The frequency and duration between shedding episodes may also vary greatly from one painted turtle to another, and will largely be reliant on such causal conditions as the amount of time spent basking, along with food and habitat conditions. As a turtle caregiver, you may have noticed an abrupt "breakage" of either small pieces or large sections of scutes from the pet's carapace, with shell casings found across the tank substrate. Do not be alarmed; this phenomenon, that occurs once, sometimes twice, or even more times in a year among certain turtles, is termed as scute shedding.

As its caregiver, there is little, if anything, that can be undertaken to alter the scute shedding process in your turtle. This natural process may need a week to achieve completion; some painted turtles, however, may seem to shed for months at a time – it is important to know that either of these shedding instances are normal and should arouse no concern. So long as the newly— developed scutes possess a smooth appearance and texture, and a vibrantly developing hue, scute shedding is a relatively ailment-free phenomenon that should not be confused with shell-related injuries suffered by the turtle.

It is an ideal combination of basking periods during the day, sufficient mineral and vitamin levels in the food needed for shell maintenance and a favorable housing set-up that encourages healthy scute shedding among your turtles. Setting up the ideal habitat and lifestyle, and then encouraging your turtle to rid itself of its old scutes at its own pace is perhaps the wisest way to trigger new scute growth without affecting the pet's health or temperament.

3 Digestive ailments

Ailment: Vomiting/Hacking cough

Symptoms: Throwing out food particles and blood through persistent cough and vomit.

Probable cause: Obstruction of food passages by large pieces of food, pieces of gravel from substrate, prolonged cough/vomiting may suggest underlying RI

Treatment: Refer to pet expert for immediate treatment, collect sample of vomit/discharge for testing, isolate pet from tank mates until recovery.

Ailment: Constipated and impacted bowel movements

Symptoms: No signs of waste collected at the bottom of the tank, sudden loss of appetite

Probable cause: Inadequate fiber content in diet,obstruction of internal passages due to ingested pebbles, gravel from substrate, cold temperatures leading to overall lethargy and inactivity.

Treatment: Place turtle in water measuring around 78 degrees Fahrenheit (32-35 degrees Celsius) for 30 minutes to help stimulate activity, ask pet expert for X- ray in case of swallowed objects, remove all objects from tank with potential to be ingested, increase fiber content in pet's diet.

Ailment: Irregularity in stoolappearance

Symptoms: Runny, liquid appearance, deviation from hard, green to brown colored appearance, presence of blood in stool

Probable cause: Disproportionate fiber, mineral, vitamin content, appearance of blood may suggest impaction as well.

Treatment: Ask pet expert for laboratory test of provided stool sample, remove all objects from tank with potential to be ingested, review and regulate content in pet's diet

Ailment: Internal parasites

Symptoms: Presence of worms or similar parasites in stool

Probable cause: Unhygienic housing conditions, contracted from open injury, other turtles, or from parasites in live feedTreatment: Immediate laboratory sample of stool, quarantine from other turtles until full recovery is made

Ailment: Blood from cloaca
Symptoms: Direct bleeding through the cloaca, or presence of blood in stool.

Probable cause: May be caused due to impaction of anal passage

Treatment: Ask pet expert for X-ray in case of swallowed objects, remove all objects from tank with potential to be ingested, increase fiber content in pet's diet.

Ailment: Aversion towards eating
Symptoms: Abrupt loss of appetite, dull/listless behavior, refusal to accept feed, lowered rate of activity, signs of brumation
Probable cause: Dependence on yolk sac immediately after hatching, decreased metabolism owing to low temperatures, monotony in diet, readiness for egg-laying, stress and trauma from previous injury/illness, underlying illness.
Treatment: Maintain consistent temperature of 75-78 degrees Fahrenheit (32-35 degrees Celsius), introduce new foods into diet, try enticing practices, separate pet from tank mates (in case of aversion to food caused by bullying incidents).

4. Other physiological ailments
Ailment: Injury/infection of eyes
Symptom: Partially/completely shut/swollen eyes, rubbing of eyes after changing of water.
Probable cause: Caused by poor housing and hygienic conditions, dehydration, deficiency of Vitamin A, underlying RI, trauma from physical injury, excessive chlorine levels in water.
Treatment: Treat swollen or shut eyes as immediate sign of

underlying illness or trauma Request for X-rays and laboratory tests to check for RI and other ailments, increase dosage of Vitamin A drops or cod-liver oil around eye area (in absence of RI),use de- chlorinated water and monitor levels, pet must be isolated from other tank mates during recovery.

Ailment: Abscess in ear
Symptom: Visible lump on one or both sides of head, inflamed, tender appearance, partially/completely shut or swollen eyes, imbalanced swimming and other impaired motor functions.
Probable cause: Bacterial infection caused by poor housing and hygiene conditions, prolonging infection from previous ailment, injury.
Treatment: Requires immediate draining of fluid from infection site, along with subsequent disinfection, difficult to treat without immediate veterinary assistance, pet must be isolated from other tank mates during recovery.

Ailment: Irregular/abnormal appearance of nails
Symptom: Overgrown or chipped nails, tender or sore around affected area, discharge from wound.
Probable cause: Injury sustained during mating, fighting or digging gravel, infection caused due to poor housing and hygiene conditions.
Treatment: Pet must be isolated from other tank mates during treatment, place turtle in dry area and administer Neosporin or Nolvasan as needed, refer to pet expert for subsequent treatment

Ailment: Stomatitis (mouth rot)
Symptom: Formation of ulcers around tongue, throat, inside and exterior of mouth area, white- yellow blisters around mouth, coughing accompanied by mucus, bleeding around mouth area.
Probable cause: Bacterial or viral infection caused by poor housing and hygiene conditions, may prove lethal if left unchecked, and will be transmitted to other tank mates.
Treatment: Requires urgent treatment of ulcers at infection site, along with disinfection, difficult to treat without immediate veterinary assistance, pet must be isolated from other tank mates

during recovery.

Ailment: Intestinal and/or reproductive prolapse
Symptom: Appearance of intestinal and/or reproductive organs from cloaca with inability to retract unaided.
Probable cause: Temporary or prolonged intestinal/reproductive disorder, injury sustained during mating or fighting, egg binding (in females)
Treatment: Pet must be isolated from other tank mates immediately, place turtle in water measuring around 78 degrees Fahrenheit (25.5 degrees Celsius) for 30 minutes to help stimulate activity, refer to pet expert for immediate treatment.

Ailment: Fanning (penile prolapse)
Symptom: Appearance of male penis from cloaca with inability to retract unaided
Probable cause: Temporary or prolonged reproductive disorder, injury sustained during mating, fighting or swallowing gravel
Treatment: Pet must be isolated from other tank mates immediately, place turtle in water measuring around 78 degrees Fahrenheit (25.5 degrees Celsius) for 30 minutes to help stimulate activity, refer to pet expert for immediate treatment.

Ailment: Egg binding/eggs laid in water
Symptom: Swollen cloacal area, sometimes accompanied by eggs laid in water, loss of appetite, aggressive or listless behavior, intestinal prolapse or persistent digging and kicking behaviors, abrupt illness, organ failure or death.
Probable cause: Lack of calcium in the diet, absence of male to fertilize egg clutch, absence of nesting zone.
Treatment: Refer to pet expert for immediate X-ray and treatment, have retained eggs extracted, clear non-viable eggs from water, pet must be isolated from other tank mates until recovery.

5. Painted Turtles and behavioral issues
Behavioural ailment: Aggressive behavior towards tank mates/owner, persistent fighting, biting, clawing, exercising control over food/basking zones

Causal factors: Inadequate space in basking zone, inadequate space within housing area, imbalanced number of males and females in tank,arrival of new tank mate.

Suggested therapy: Provide ample completely dry space for basking, ensure privacy in case of new pets, observe dynamics with tank mates and isolate if necessary, provide necessary solitary nesting spaces for egg-laying females away from harassing males, provide separate feeding/basking timings if necessary.

Behavioural ailment: Not enough time spent basking

Causal factors: Very warm temperatures of water that discourage basking, excessively high/low temperature setting within housing area, inadequate space in basking zone, absence of heat source, stressful dynamics between tank mates, insufficient privacy

Suggested therapy: Regulate temperature of water to 75-78 degrees Fahrenheit (24-25.5 degrees Celsius) and basking area to 90-95 degrees Fahrenheit (32.2-35 degrees Celsius), provide ample completely dry space for basking, ensure privacy in case of new pets

Behavioural ailment: Excessive time spent basking, general listlessness, lowered rate of activity, lethargic movements

Causal factors: Excessively cold temperatures of water and housing, nervousness if newly acquired, bullying from other tank mates, possible underlying respiratory infection

Suggested therapy: Observe dynamics with tank mates and isolate if necessary, increase water temperature to 75-78 degrees Fahrenheit (24-25.5 degrees Celsius), refer to pet expert for necessary tests and X- rays, provide adequate privacy and conditions in case of new pet.

Behavioural ailment: Restless behavior, agitated appearance and movements

Causal factors: Insufficient adjustment time (in case of new pet), inadequate temperature settings, stress due to previous of underlying illness, readiness to lay eggs (in case of female), incorrect handling from owner

Suggested therapy: Regulate temperature of water to 75-78 degrees Fahrenheit (24-25.5 degrees Celsius) and basking area to 90-95 degrees Fahrenheit (32.2-35 degrees Celsius), observe dynamics with tank mates and isolate if necessary, provide adequate privacy and conditions in case of new pet, provide necessary nesting spaces for egg-laying females.

Behavioural ailment: Erratic movements, unnatural movements while swimming, walking, unbalanced gait, circular movements
Causal factors: Fluid buildup in lungs, respiratory infection, probable ear infection, inconsistent temperature settings within the tank, stressful dynamics between tank mates, insufficient privacy.
Suggested therapy: Observe dynamics with tank mates and isolate if necessary, Provide adequate privacy and conditions in case of new pet, regulate temperature of water to 75-78 degrees Fahrenheit (24-25.5 degrees Celsius), check for probable ear or respiratory infections and provide necessary treatment

6. Treating common Painted Turtle ailments
Treating superficial shell injuries:

When you notice a crack or bump, or feel an irregularity around the carapace or plastron area of your painted turtle, your immediate course of action should be to separate your pet from its tank mates, then and closely inspect the terrapin for signs of bleeding. New injuries to the shell may or may not ooze blood, making the gravity of the injury difficult to ascertain unless treatment is started. To effectively treat a superficial bleeding injury impacting your painted turtle:

● Isolate the turtle in a sterile plastic storage container for immediate diagnosis and treatment. If your turtle resists being handled, you can safeguard yourself against aggressive bites by putting a wad of soft towel or cloth in your pet's mouth.

● Use a thick, clean towel to dab on the affected area, and apply slight pressure on the affected shell surface to contain the bleeding.

● Once the bleeding has either subsided or completely stopped, only then should you begin medication. Safe antibacterial soaps and disinfectants include Betadine and Hibiclens, easily sourced from most local pharmacies and pet care suppliers.

● Fill a large bowl with lukewarm water, no hotter, and then gently lower your turtle into the bowl. With the help of a sterile brush with soft bristles, apply the disinfectant on to the affected area, firmly holding your pet in place as you massage the area with water and medicine.

● After the bath, place your pet back into the dry temporary storage tub for three to four hours, giving the terrapin's wonder time to heal and repair. Repeat the medicinal bath once the next day, continuing the routine until your painted turtle's injury has healed.

● Apart from the obvious signs of bleeding, a grave injury to the carapace or plastron area is also revealed through a strong, foul smell, an unnaturally tender shell-texture or discoloration that deviates from the pet's regular markings. If the affected area exhibits any of these signs at any point before or during the first-aid process, it is best to rush your painted turtle to the veterinarian.

● No matter how little the injury or cut it is best to monitor its healing on a daily basis, and contact your exotic pet expert in case the injury worsens or becomes infected.

Treating minor cuts, wounds and attacks from predators:

Treatments will not only have to be administered for shell-related injuries, but also other physical wounds that will impact your painted turtle. These may include cuts, scratches, nips, bites or slightly deeper injuries caused due to sharp objects inside or outside the tank, fights with tank mates or attacks from predators in the surrounding area. As in the case of treating shell-related injuries, it is important that your painted turtle is at ease in your presence, and is held securely within your hold. If the pet tries to strike you in defense or strongly resists your tactics to subdue them, it may only agitate their injuries.

1. **Predatory terrain: Terrestrial predators**
   Common predators (eggs): Garter snakes, Chipmunks, 13-lined ground and gray squirrels, groundhogs, raccoons, badgers, gray and red fox, humans
   Common predators (hatchlings/adults): Weasels, musk rats, minks, raccoons, alligators, copperhead snakes, racer snakes, rice rats.

2. **Predatory terrain: Aerial predators**
   Common predators (eggs): Crows
   Common predators (hatchlings/adults): Red-shouldered hawks, crows, bald eagles, osprey.

3. **Predatory terrain: Marine predators**
   Common predators (eggs): n/a
   Common predators (hatchlings/adults): Water bugs, bass, catfish, bull frogs, snapping turtles, water snakes, herons.

● Isolate the turtle in a sterile plastic storage container for immediate diagnosis and treatment. If your turtle resists being handled, you can safeguard yourself against aggressive bites by putting a wad of soft towel or cloth in your pet's mouth.

● If your turtle has either lost consciousness or has entered a state of shock, do not attempt to make it swim. Check instead for any sings of bleeding or a serious ailment, such as a fractured limb.

● Use a thick, clean towel to dab on the affected area, and apply slight pressure on the affected shell surface to contain the bleeding.

● Once the bleeding has either subsided or completely stopped, only then should you begin medication. Safe antibacterial soaps and disinfectants include Betadine and Hibiclens, easily sourced from most local pharmacies and pet care suppliers.

• Fill a large bowl with lukewarm water, no hotter, and then gently lower your turtle into the bowl. With the help of a sterile brush with soft bristles, apply the disinfectant on to the affected area, firmly holding your pet in place as you massage the area with water and medicine.

• After the bath, place your pet back into the dry temporary storage tub for three to four hours, giving the terrapin's wonder time to heal and repair. Repeat the medicinal bath once the next day, continuing the routine until your painted turtle's injury has healed.

• In case of attacks from predators, apart from administering first aid and taking subsequent veterinary action, it is also important that you isolate the injured chelonian from its tank members. This will prevent such instances as bullying episodes from healthy tank mates, or the spread of infection from the injured turtle to other inhabitants.

• No matter how minor the injury or cut, it is best to monitor its recovery, and contact your exotic pet expert in case the wound becomes more serious or infected.

Treating Painted turtles in case of drowning:

It may seem bizarre or even impossible, but painted turtles, just like other chelonians, are prone to drowning, especially in a captive setting with improper aquatic and terrestrial conditions. Adept swimmers by nature, drowning is usually initiated only if a turtle has turned over on its shell while in water and does not have adequate space or physical stamina to right itself.

In immediate need of oxygen once overturned, painted turtles will temporarily brumate as a precautionary measure, waiting for assistance. They may start sinking to the bottom of the tank, but will still be breathing for some time, and can be resuscitated if taken out of the water immediately. While an urgent visit to the local exotic pet expert should be arranged for, here are some first-aid measures that can take your turtle out of the danger zone:

● Never try to place a drowning turtle on its back once out of the water, as this act may further constrict the clogged air passages and lungs, killing your pet.

● Grasp your turtle by the neck, clasping at the base of the skull behind its ears. Then, stretch the neck out as far as possible.

● Next, release excess liquid from the lung area by holding the turtle with its head pointed downwards and tail pointing upward. Ensure that your clasp on the neck is firm throughout.

● Gently place your turtle on its belly on a broad flat surface, while maintaining your grip around the neck.

● Now, stand in front of your turtle (facing its head), and clasp and extend its front legs in your direction as far as possible.

● Next, hold its legs straight and thrust them backwards into its chest, taking care not to bend its limbs at the elbow joints. Repeat this back-and-forth pumping action to help the turtle sputter out any remaining liquid.

● As soon as the excess water has been thrust out, rush your turtle to your local veterinary hospital to begin such therapies as oxygen supply and a possible dose of antibiotics (in case your turtle has contracted pneumonia in the process). Some owners have claimed success by practicing straw-to-mouth breathing as a means of immediate oxygen supply. This method, though sound in theory, has not yet been verified for accuracy and is not a substitute for expert veterinary attention. It is the speed and accuracy of your actions that can help prevent drowning and save your turtle's life.

Knowing when to seek external medical assistance

Most illnesses and ailments that will befall your painted turtles will likely be caused by irregularities in their diet, unsuitable housing conditions or stress caused by a number of factors. As a poikilothermic exotic species, painted turtle turtles in captivity deserve protection against ailments and infections owing to the vast differences between their captive environment and natural habitat. While health care for this terrapin may require slightly more time and effort than that provided to a dog or cat, your involvement in ensuring your pet's optimum health will benefit you as well.

In many cases, superficial shell injuries and bruises can be treated at home, without seeking external medical assistance. As long as your painted turtle is swimming robustly, has a coordinated gait, is feeding and basking at regular intervals, is active and not displaying signs of if listlessness or stress, medical attention may involve little more than separating the pet from its tank mates for two or three days, while providing the right medication or behavior therapy.

A minor cold or injury, should not greatly affect the behavior or daily routine of your terrapin in any drastic way. Painted turtles will only exhibit erratic behavior and overt signs of physical discomfort when they have been affected by a grave underlying medical condition. Should your pet exhibit an abrupt shift in behavioral patterns or motor function, or suffer medical trauma, it becomes important to contact your veterinarian at the earliest.

If your painted turtle is in need of urgent expert medical attention, it will display such symptoms as:

• Blood from the cloaca,

• A seizure episode,

• Partial or total abrupt paralysis,

• Sudden or constant discharge from the eyes or ears,

• Loss of or partial or complete limb (due to injury).

Your terrapin may not always display signs that are physical manifestations of an unobvious illness. In some cases, illnesses such as Metabolic Bone Disease and Respiratory infections may only be hinted at by observing the reptile's motor functions and behavioral symptoms for at least 24-48 hours. If your chelonian displays the following signs for over 48 hours, it is best to rush it to your exotic pet expert at the earliest:

● Prolonged loss of appetite,
● Pink or red patches or spots under the shell surface,
● Abscesses around the ears,
● Refusal to eat or bask,
● Discharge from nose or eyes,
● Dull, listless behavior.
● Irregular and erratic swimming/movement patterns

In order to prepare your herpetological expert to provide the right type of treatment for your pet, it is advisable that you call ahead and intimate the medical staff of your painted turtle's emergency. In cases of immediate surgery or drowning, such arrangements as oxygen supply and an operation room will have to be freed and readied in advance. Calling ahead also allows the medical staff to direct you to another health care facility, should your veterinarian not be present at the time of the emergency. Collect and carry such samples as stool, vomit and shed skin or shell components if possible, to help your veterinarian diagnose and advise treatment for your pet with speed and accuracy.

7. Preventing health concerns for your Painted Turtle

If you are the type of caregiver who is attentive, thoughtful, quick-acting and committed, then you most likely will already have a daily routine that is mindful of your Painted turtle's needs. In an ideal environment that gives the terrapin the ideal food, housing, basking, swimming and hygiene conditions, there is little chance that your pet will incur anything more serious than the odd fight-related injury or scruff to the shell.

No matter how prepared you may feel at treating an illness if it should occur, it is always better to take every precautionary measure necessary to safeguard your chelonian against the possibility of disease. Not only are all ailments physically strenuous for the terrapin, but several infections sustained by your pet may also spread to other tank mates. Here are a few ways by which you can ensure the health and well-being of your pet:

1. A daily inspection of your painted turtle's substrate for food remains and excrement is not only preferable, it is also essential. As adults, these chelonians eat generously, shed equally copious amounts of excrement, and create a mess that could quickly contaminate an enclosed space.

2. Any kind of live feed whose remains could decay and compost, along with all the excrement, should be cleaned out once daily.

3. The water will be filtered for the most part with your installed systems, but will still need to be changed once every 30-45 days. The substrate and flooring within the tank, if provided, will also have to be replaced once every 3-6 months. This will avoid the possibility of any infestations from rotting and decaying matter.

4. It is best to avoid putting in such items as small, easy-to-swallow stones, twigs, gravel and allergens such as sawdust into the tank. Since painted turtles are curious and slightly greedy creatures, they may try to eat objects they do not understand, leading to possible choking hazards and internal injuries.

5. Poikilothermic by nature, painted turtles thrive best when housed in regulated temperatures and conditions that mimic their natural surroundings. They become easily stressed if the temperature within their housing is either susceptible to erratic shifts, or is beyond their adaptability range. As chelonians, a consistent water temperature of 75-78 degrees Fahrenheit (24-25.5 degrees Celsius) and basking area temperature of 90-95 degrees Fahrenheit (32.2-35 degrees Celsius) for adults, while maintaining the same in the winter months will keep your terrapins safe from the hazards of abrupt hibernation or stressful behavior.

6. Ensure that you provide a designated and separate zone for basking activities, and equipt it in a way that complements your turtle's diurnal nature. Provide a basking platform that easily accommodates all tank mates even if they stack up on each other vertically, and ensure that the platform is as dry as possible. Supplement the basking zone with adequate heating and lighting fixtures, while ensuring the basking area is injury-and-escape-proof.

7. Develop an interest and be alert towards the interaction of your painted turtles with other tank mates, members in your house and their immediate surroundings. These terrapins are expressive by nature and will display aggressive and defensive behaviors or obvious symptoms of trauma when faced with injury or a perceived threat.

8. In case of newly acquired painted turtles in a community setting, set aside a probationary period between 60-90 days for the new terrapin in a solitary and clean tank or container. This allows the turtle to acclimatize itself to its surroundings, lowers risks of being bullied by older members in the community and allows you to ascertain the health of the new pet.

9. Finally, closely monitor your role as the primary source of food for the terrapins, along with the amount of food needed by your pets. Plan and prepare a diet that contains a healthy proportion of live feed, turtle pellets, aquatic plants and necessary vegetation, and ensure a steady supply of calcium, phosphorus, Vitamin D3 and other essential nutrients.

8. The importance of Veterinary care

Trained, friendly and knowledgeable though they may be, veterinarians who specialize in such conventional pets as cats, dogs, rabbits, hamsters or other livestock may not always be the best choice to treat your cold-blooded pond-sliding reptilians. These poikilothermic chelonians demand a separate school of knowledge and care from chelonian experts who have trained in, and are familiar with the physiology, anatomy and behavior of painted turtles. The good news is, finding an exotic reptile pet health expert in your local area is no longer a trial-and-error process, but one made easy through technological advancement and the growing popularity of turtles as household pets.

If you do not already have a veterinary herpetological expert to contact, your painted turtle vendors or breeders will usually be willing to assist you. Breeders and retailers often know the best doctors and veterinary care teams in the area, since the health of their terrapins is their top priority. If the options they provide are not convenient for you, however, some simple research of your own will yield plenty of results.

Most experts offering exotic pet and reptilian health care services in today's times offer their services on such public platforms as the Internet and can be located by entering the right key words into your search engine. Additionally, you can also browse through feedback and reviews from other breeders and owners to narrow down trusted herpetological experts for your Painted turtles.

Once you find a pet expert who best meets your requirements, arrange for your pet to visit their office for an initial examination. To avoid prolonged interaction between your terrapins and unfavorable conditions such as strangers or unhygienic conditions, and to provide quick treatment for your pet, you should also aim to find an expert who is willing to make house calls. Many veterinarians, if trained correctly, understand the relative complications involved in transporting a large group of aquatic reptiles in a cramped vehicle, and will be more than willing to oblige you. Ultimately, it is the bond you form with your herpetological expert that will ensure your pet receives the best possible medical care.

9. Providing insurance for your Painted Turtle

Animals such as painted turtles are termed exotic pets since they require extremely rigid standards for housing, diet and health care for a life that is without any fatal complications or ailments. Despite your best efforts and wishes, however, it may not always be easy, or even possible to provide the daily rigorous level of care that your terrapins demand; it is tricky to ascertain exactly how many turtle pellets and live feed constitute the ideal composition for their daily diet, and additionally complicated to regulate and replicate factors needed for brumation and basking.

It is perhaps owing to such causal factors, that painted turtles who do succumb to ailments often find themselves victims of relapses and long-term diligent care. A painted turtle who contracts a respiratory infection, for instance, may have a weak immune system and may be constantly affected by changes in the water or ambient temperature; another pet with shell-related conditions such as MBD or digestive disorders may need regular medical supervision and rounds of laboratory tests. Assuring proper veterinary care for each ailment that befalls your terrapin throughout its lifespan can, therefore, quickly become an expensive affair.

To help protect you financially while safeguarding your terrapin's interests, countries like the United States, Canada and the United Kingdom offer health insurance policies for a variety of domestic animals, ranging from household pets to livestock, including exotic pet reptiles such as painted turtles. Healthcare and medical plans drafted and planned by these companies provide an umbrella of financial cover for such cases as shell-related ailments, respiratory, cardiac and intestinal diseases, rectal issues, vaccinations and even cancer. There even exist such insurance companies that readily provide customized insurance plans for your pets, based on your chelonian's needs and your payment flexibility.

In the United States, pet insurance policies are offered by such companies as Pet Assure and Nationwide Pet Insurance. In the United Kingdom, you can find pet insurance policies with companies like Exotic Direct and Cliverton.

Chapter 8: Breeding Painted Turtles

Several people like to bring home painted Turtles mainly for breeding purposes. While the intention is usually to restore the number of turtles in the environment or to make a quick buck, it is very important for owners to understand how to breed painted turtles correctly. This will ensure that the offsprings are healthy. In addition to this, managing the delicate hatchlings can be a challenge for most people. So, if you are even remotely considering breeding make sure you do your homework well.

1.   Understanding the risks of painted turtle breeding in captivity

If you have hatched a successful clutch of painted turtles in captivity, please take a moment to truly appreciate and celebrate your hard work. It is considered among the most challenging tasks to maintain the natural optimal nesting and incubation patterns in an artificial environment; that you have done so is a testament to your commitment. However, before you undertake this arduous task, it is wise to consider the amount of factors that surround the breeding and subsequent care for painted turtle hatchlings during each phase of the endeavor.

To begin with, breeding your painted turtles can be easily perfected with time and practice; this ease in routine could leave you with an uncontrollable rise in your personal hatchling population. Once hatched, the infants will require a specific environment within which to grow comfortably; any deviation or fluctuation from the accepted conditions could result in the death of the young ones.

Should you be able to successfully hatch the eggs, it then adds to your responsibility – and expenses – to provide a housing that allows them to develop through each stage of growth. This will include buying a number of tanks, changing the water constantly, doubling up on splitting feeding and cleaning duties between the adults and babies and installing new filtering, heating and lighting devices, to name a few. The hatchlings may also never be accepted by the adult community, than requiring you to maintain separate housing areas.

There is then the future problem of long-term care for the hatchlings. If successfully raised to their adult stage, you will have plenty of terrapins who survive and will need to be cared for till you can provide alternate housing for them. You can choose to sell them to interested individuals, or choose to sell them to a local reputed vendor, but these practices will have to be permitted and legal within your residence. Indeed, the entire process of breeding your adults or hatching the eggs, whether for personal use or profit, is futile without legal permits from the concerned authorities, and is definitely not permitted in some states in North America.

Any feelings of dissatisfaction with the pet in terms of care, or feeling overwhelmed at the overall costs and work that goes into raising such a large group of painted turtles may then prompt you or the new owners to either consider giving them up for adoption or releasing them into the wild. As members of a readily breeding, yet slightly invasive species family, we now understand that this procedure may not only be traumatic for their welfare, but is also discouraged in several areas around the world. On a personal note, this endeavor, rewarding though it may be, will consume a large part of your free time, and require dedication, patience and support from the legal bodies at every stage. Each phase of the breeding process will also affect the people you live with, whether financially, emotionally and even physically, making it essential that they are cooperative of your plans. When you do decide to breed your painted turtles, take the time to consider the circumstances surrounding their breeding, and the number of factors you leave to chance – it will help you make a decision that works out for you.

2. Caring for the Eggs
Incubation and Hatching

Natural Incubation

A seemingly natural choice for the incubation of your turtle eggs once hatched would be to allow the mother incubate and hatch the eggs herself. In the wild, a female painted turtle likes to dig up nesting spots deep into the soil to deposit her clutch of eggs for safe hatching. In captivity, she will look for similar nesting zones, signalling her readiness to lay eggs with frantic digging activity.

If you have provided a specific nesting zone for your pet, it is here that she will lay the eggs. An ideal nesting area would be at least 12 inches deep and contain a substrate made of organic compost soil and loamy sand in equal proportions. While looking for the perfect nest, the mothers prefer those spots that are free of such sharp objects and particles as gravel or stones. Ensure that your substrate is free of abrasive material to prevent egg binding, egg laying in water, or injury to your female.

After the female has laid her clutch, successful natural incubation should result in the eggs hatching between 70 to 80 days. In the event that your housing area is not suitable for natural incubation and hatching, you can provide the eggs with artificial incubation.

Artificial Incubation

Collecting turtle eggs for artificial incubation requires slightly different handling than collecting poultry or fowl eggs would. From the moment they are laid, the eggs should be handled with utmost care, without being turned, shaken or placed in any other position. Those eggs that were laid in water and not collected immediately would have become non-viable, and are best disposed of.

The entire process of incubation takes up to 80 days, and you can find many commercially manufactured incubators that correctly serve this purpose. Incubating painted turtle eggs is a tricky procedure that requires specific temperature and humidity settings. Specifically-designed commercial incubators solve this problem by allowing you to regulate conditions with an inbuilt thermostat. For an economic option, a sturdy plastic container filled with vermiculite (to replicate natural nesting zone), drilled with strategically placed holes for ventilation will comfortably incubate your clutch.

The most interesting feature of artificial incubation is that it allows you to regulate the temperature of the nesting zone to determine what sex your hatchlings will be. Owing to the unique phenomena of gender determination via climatic temperatures, a temperature on the lower end of the accepted spectrum will give you male hatchlings, higher temperatures will hatch females, and a median transitory temperature may also result in transgender turtles!

3. Caring for the young

Even though you may undertake the incubation process with utmost care and caution, you still should not be disappointed if all the eggs don't hatch, or if they do, and the hatchlings do not survive. Painted turtle eggs, in captivity, have a slighter accelerated rate of hatching if undertaken carefully, but it is the complication in the subsequent care provided to the infant that raises their mortality rate as well.

Brooding zones for hatchlings are critical to their survival, whether they have hatched through the artificial or natural incubation method. You should shift the hatchlings into the infant housing set-up almost as soon as they hatch; this brooder can be a commercially manufactured predetermined one, or even a makeshift aquarium or container set up to house hatchlings.

Ensure that the brooding zone is housed away from direct light, heat, or wind. Adequate UVA and UVB lighting, along with a submersible water heater will also have to be fixed. A basking zone in a separate area should also be maintained for optimal growth; maintain the temperature of the water at 80 degrees Fahrenheit (26.6 degrees Celsius) and the basking areas at 90 degrees Fahrenheit (32.3 degrees Celsius). The water will also need to be supplemented with a filtration system, and cleaned out at least once a month.

While it is tricky to determine the exact moment of hatching, in an artificial setting, keeping a constant eye on the eggs between the 70th and 80th days will usually reward you with the sight of a hatchling Painted turtle. They may, however, still be feeding off the contents of the yolk sac; if noticed on the hatchling plastron, allow the young one to dispose of the sac itself.

New-born hatchlings survive best when fed with a specially-curated carnivorous starter diet, prepared to contain all the necessary nutrients, especially shell, bone and muscle building protein. The transition to a more herbivorous diet, such as vegetation and aquatic plants, is usually completed by the time the hatchling reaches crosses a year in age. Some hatchlings may show an aversion to food at first, but can be enticed to feed and accept live feed and pellets.

During the first months of development, painted hatchlings are best left undisturbed; any excessive handling could cause injury or stress to the terrapin. As long as you make timely calm appearances to provide food and clean the tank, your hatchlings, in time, should grow to recognize you as their caregiver.

There is no hard evidence that advocates one method of hatching over the other. While the natural way seems like the best hatching technique, an artificial method of incubation may prove just as successful, provided these practices are permitted by the governing authorities in your area. The final choice to hatch Painted turtles truly comes down your individual settings, preferences and expectations from your pets.

Chapter 9: The Complete Painted Turtle Care Shopping List

The following list comprises all the items you will need to care for your painted turtle on a daily basis - from housing to diet, including accessories and healthcare items. Most of these products will be available at your local pet stores, whether in the United States, Canada or the United Kingdom. Several companies also offer pet equipment and accessories for sale through online retail websites, or via marketplaces on popular and reputed breeder websites. In the United States and Canada, you can access Petco, PetSmart, Pet Mountain or That Pet Place to find items that address your exotic pet care needs, while Exotic Pets, Online Reptile Shop, 888 Reptiles and Rainforest Supplies, offers the same services in the United Kingdom.

Housing
Glass tank, preferably with capacity between 50 and 85 gallons (for pair of Painted turtles housed for breeding) or Plastic Storage Tub or Plastic Outdoor Storage Pool
Cabinet, Brackets
Water Filters (such as Rena FilStar or AquaClear)
Water heaters - Submersible (100 or 200 watt, preferably 1 pair)
Basking platform (Zoo Med Turtle dock or Acrylic Turtle ramp)
Heating lamps (with ceramic/porcelain sockets, amount depending on the size of the tank and number of turtles)
Ceramic Heat Emitter (100 watt)
Fluorescent UVA/UVB bulbs (such as ReptiSun 10.0)
Pet-bedding (such as Burgess, ProRep or Pebbels and Gravel bags from Lowe's)
Electric timer
Large fish net
Wire/mesh screen
Water conditioning/testing kit

Diet
Fruits and Vegetables
Red lettuce leaf
Apples
Mustard leaf
Bell pepper
Nectarines
Blackberries
Oranges
Broccoli
Papaya
Collard greens
Turnip leaves
Carrot tops
Peaches
Cauliflower
Prickly Pears
Cherries
Pineapple
Chicory
Plums
Cranberries
Cucumber
Raspberries
Endives
Green lettuce leaf
Romaine lettuce leaves
Sprouts
Grapes
Strawberries
Honeydew melon
Watermelon
Kale
Mangoes
Flowers and plants
Duckweed
Water hyacinth
Water lettuce

Frog-bit
Anacharis
Pondweed
Water Starwort
Water Milofil
Nasturtium
Amazon Swords
Water Lily
Water Fern
Hornwort
Dandelion
Live feed
Earthworms
Superworms
Feeder fish
Guppies
Rosy-red minnows
Daphnia
Chicken
Turkey
Crickets
Shrimp (Gammarus)
Krill
Silkworms
Waxworms
Mosquito larvae
Pond snail
Tadpoles
Apple snail
Tubifex worms
Mealworms
Miscellaneous food items
Commercial-brand turtle pellets (FLuker's Aquatic Turtle Diet, Nasco Turtle Brittle, Tetra ReptoMin, Mazuri Freshwater Turtle Diet, etc.)
Boiled eggs
Brined shrimp/krill
Canned de-shelled snails

Healthcare
Cuttlefish bone
RepCal
Repti Turtle Sulfa Dip
Vitamin A Drops
Neosporin
Nolvasan
Betadine
Hibiclens
Baytril
Toothbrushes
Thermometers
Canned de-shelled snails

Healthcare
Cuttlefish bone
RepCal
Repti Turtle Sulfa Dip
Vitamin A Drops
Neosporin
Nolvasan
Betadine
Hibiclens
Baytril
Toothbrushes
Thermometers

Conclusion

Now that you are equipped with all the information that you need with respect to the painted turtle, I am sure that you will make a great owner. It takes a lot of initial work to keep this reptile at home, with the right set-up matched by a continued commitment towards your turtle's care. While that may sound intimidating, if you are unable to meet all the requirements and needs of your pets, you will only compromise on their health and well-being. To conclude, I would like to remind you that raising a painted turtle is a big financial undertaking.

Here is a breakdown of the approximate costs of keeping a Painted turtle:

- Tank: $150 to $450 or £100 to £300
- Bedding: $6 to $30 or £4 to £20
- Feed: $4 to $10 or £3 to £7 for a 2 pound bag
- Water filters and testing kits: $60 to $175 or £40 to £120
- Heating: $30 to $65 or £20 to £40
- Lighting: $60 to $175 or £40 to £120
- Veterinary Care: $20 to $150 or £15 to £100

Once you are sure of making this commitment, you can convert your home into a great place for your painted turtle. I hope this book answers all your questions about having painted turtle.

References

Important: please check out the websites and breeders thoroughly. Be aware that there are a lot of cowboys trading on the web.

The websites mentioned in this book were active at the time of printing. However, by the time you read this book, the websites might no longer be active. That, of course, is out of my control as the Internet changes rapidly.

Seek to continually learn more about your painted turtle. As with the care of all exotic pets, new techniques, strategies and concepts in such areas as housing, diet, health care and breeding are discovered and implemented at a rapid rate. Never turn down an opportunity to learn more about your new pets, and eagerly seek out those who may know more than you do about these temperamental yet fascinating reptiles.

1. Books

Practical Encyclopedia of Keeping and Breeding Freshwater Turtles and Tortoises

By A.C. Highfield

Turtles of the United States and Canada

By Carl H. Ernst, Jeffrey E. Lovich and Roger W. Barbour

A Field Guide to Reptiles and Amphibians of Eastern and Central North America

Expanded by Roger Conant and Joseph T. Collins

Houghton Mifflin Company, 3rd Edition

Keeping and Breeding Freshwater Turtles

By Ross Gurley

2. Websites

In the information age, learning more about your painted turtle is only a few clicks away. Be sure to bookmark these sites for quick access in the future.

Informational Websites

Turtle Forum

http://www.turtleforum.com

This website and message board contains plenty of information about Painted turtle care and handling.

Turtles and Turtle Care

www.turtles.net

Turtles provides extensive knowledge on several types of chelonians, including the various breeds of painted turtle.

Austin's Turtle Page

http://www.austinsturtlepage.com

A popular website with a thriving community forum featuring news, information and more concerning Painted turtle and other common exotics.

All Turtles

http://www.allturtles.com

Information about most turtles native to North America. This site provides identification photos from most species and tips for spotting various species in the wild.

RepticZone

http://www.repticzone.com

This website provides a variety of helpful resources, as well as information about painted turtlecare and purchase. You can also use this website to find information on breed standards, exotic pet fairs and meet other reptile enthusiasts.

Turtle Times

http://www.turtletimes.com

Another popular website with a thriving community forum featuring news, information and more concerning painted turtle and other common exotics.

Breeders

Painted turtle breeders are not only an excellent source for purchasing hatchlings; they can also provide a wealth of information through detailed and interactive forums posted on the Internet. At the time of writing, all the following links were active and functional; in the event that any source should re-direct you to an inactive page, please understand that the maintenance of these websites is subject to Internet-policies and the preferences of the website owners; we cannot claim personal responsibility for the same.

The Turtle Source

http://www.theturtlesource.com

The Turtle Source sells hatchlings and eggs of painted turtle and many other poultry breeds.

Backwater Reptiles

http://www.backwaterreptiles.com

Backwater Reptiles houses a variety of chelonian species, and their website provides information about painted turtle housing, maintenance and feeding.

Reptile City

http://www.reptilecity.com

Reptile City is another go-to website for lesser-common exotic reptile species, and their website provides information about Painted turtle housing, maintenance and feeding.

University and Governmental Resources

Indiana Department of Natural Resources

http://www.in.gov/dnr/fishwild

Primarily focused on wildlife and flora, this website contains plenty of information about painted turtles.

Massachusetts Legalities on Painted turtle Ownership

http://www.mass.gov/eea/docs/agr/animal-health/pet-shop-licensing/new-requirements-for-exotic-animals-sold-in-pet-shops.pdf

This website has comprehensive information on the painted turtle along with other local wildlife. In addition to reading about the painted turtle, you can also learn about their predators, prey and competitors here.

Michigan Department of Natural Resources

http://www.michigan.gov/dnr/0,1607,7-153-10370_12145_12201-60649--,00.html

This page, provided and maintained by the Michigan State government, contains a wealth of data concerning all common local reptiles, including the painted turtle.

The Centre for Disease Control and Prevention

http://www.cdc.gov

Based in Atlanta, Georgia, the CDC provides information on a variety of diseases that may be zoonotic. Additionally, the website provides further resources for coping with outbreaks of salmonella.

Veterinary Resources

Veterinarians.com

http://www.localvets.com

This site is a search engine that can help you find a local veterinarian to treat your painted turtle.

Holly House Vets

http://www.hollyhousevets.co.uk

A comprehensive website that covers various subjects like life history, care and breeding of different red-eared sliders, along with relevant veterinary resources in the UK.

Heartland Veterinary

http://www.heartlandveterinary.com

A comprehensive website that covers various subjects like life history, care and breeding of different red-eared sliders, along with relevant veterinary resources in the UK.

1/17

CPSIA information can be obtained
at www.ICGtesting.com
Printed in the USA
LVOW13s1729190117
521538LV00011B/922/P